# IN AN
# ITALIAN KITCHEN

*With 125 delicious*
*authentic recipes*

FOOD PHOTOGRAPHY BY PETER BARRY AND NEIL SUTHERLAND
DESIGNED BY SALLY STRUGNELL AND ALISON JEWELL
RECIPES SELECTED AND EDITED BY JILLIAN STEWART

CLB 2468
© 1991 Colour Library Books Ltd, Godalming, Surrey, England.
All rights reserved.
This 1991 edition published by Arch Cape Press,
distributed by Outlet Book Company, Inc, a Random House Company,
225 Park Avenue South, New York, New York 10003.
Colour Separations by Advance Laser Graphic Arts, Hong Kong
Printed and Bound in Italy
ISBN 0 517 02549 3
8 7 6 5 4 3 2 1

# IN AN ITALIAN KITCHEN

*With 125 delicious authentic recipes*

## ARCH CAPE PRESS
### NEW YORK

# CONTENTS

First page: Anchovy Pâté with Crudités. Previous
pages: the Doge's Palace in Venice, a great attraction
for tourists. Inset: a colorful pasta dish, using the best
of Italian ingredients. These pages: Lazise harbor on
Lake Garda. Overleaf: Zuppa Inglese.

If the mention of Italian cooking conjures up images in your mind of pasta, pizza and little else, *In an Italian Kitchen* will surprise you by revealing the different flavors, colors and textures that give true Italian cuisine its very distinct – and tasty – character.

To discover all the style and virtuosity of Italian cooking this book takes the cook on a journey through Italy's rugged countryside to its spectacular cities giving a unique insight into the character of Italy, its people and its cuisine.

Thanks to its favorable geography and climate, Italy has an abundance of fresh produce, from vegetables and fruit to cheeses and seafood. Italian cooking does not therefore rely on either expensive ingredients or ornate presentation, but rather on making delicious use of these simple, but good-quality, ingredients. Many of these ingredients are probably already in your store cupboard. If, however, you intend to cook "Italian style" on a regular basis, it is important to remember that vegetables and fruit should always be of the highest possible quality and should be bought regularly, in small quantities, to ensure they are fresh and crisp – many Italians shop daily to ensure that they are getting the best and freshest available produce.

Pasta – that great Italian favorite – is often freshly made in many Italian homes, but as it is somewhat difficult to prepare, you may find it much more convenient to buy the fresh variety from your local delicatessen. A wide range of dried, packaged varieties are now on offer, but these do not match the taste of the real thing! Cheeses such as Parmesan, ricotta and mozzarella are crucial components of many Italian dishes and the best place to find the various cheeses used in these recipes is also your local delicatessen, although many can also now be found in good supermarkets.

Herbs are another integral part of Italian cooking, lending their own subtle yet distinctive flavor to many classic dishes. This flavor is always best if you either grow your own herbs, or to buy them fresh. The most commonly used varieties are basil, oregano, marjoram, rosemary, bay leaf and thyme, not forgetting garlic of course – an indispensable ingredient in the Italian kitchen.

When you eat "Italian style," whether it's at home or in an Italian restaurant, the meal should be a sociable event. Italian life is very family orientated and mealtimes are always occasions for people to meet and talk, whether it is over a leisurely lunch or a relaxing evening meal. The food is usually accompanied with local Italian wines or mineral water. The menu may include soup, antipasto (hors d'oeuvres), pasta, risotto, or possibly a meat dish (often veal or chicken), with a variety of vegetables or a salad, and there is usually fresh fruit or a piece of cheese to finish off the meal. Desserts such as ice cream or ricotta pancakes, cakes and chocolates tend to be reserved either for special occasions or for visits to coffee houses, but a large selection of favorites has been included here for you to concoct at home.

So why not turn yours into an Italian kitchen and discover the delights of good cooking and stylish eating for yourself. *Buon appetito*!

# Chapter 1
# SOUPS AND APPETIZERS

## EGGPLANT APPETIZER

Eggplants are extremely versatile and can be combined with a whole variety of other ingredients with delicious results.

Preparation Time: 15 minutes
Cooking Time: 20 minutes
Serves: 4

### INGREDIENTS

*1 large eggplant*
*2 ripe tomatoes, peeled, seeded and chopped*
*2 cloves garlic, minced*
*¼ cup oil*
*1 tbsp tomato paste*
*¼ cup water*
*Salt*
*Pepper*

### METHOD

Cut eggplant lengthwise into strips ¼ inch × 2½ inches. Heat oil in pan until hot. Add the eggplant and cook for 5 minutes or until cooked. Remove from pan with slotted spoon. Add extra oil as necessary and heat. Fry garlic for 30 seconds. Add the tomatoes, tomato paste, salt and pepper, and water and cook for 10 minutes or until sauce is thick. Add the eggplant and stir together. Adjust seasoning and cook for a further 5 minutes. Serve hot or cold.

Previous pages: the church and campanile, or bell tower, of San Giorgio Maggiore in Venice. Right: the twelfth-century tower of Damecuta, part of the Villa of the Emperor Tiberius, on Capri's northwest coast.

## TOMATO SOUP

No book on Italian cooking would be complete without a recipe for tomato soup. Perfect fare for any time of the year.

Preparation Time: 15 minutes
Cooking Time: 45 minutes
Serves: 4

### INGREDIENTS

*1lb ripe tomatoes*
*1 carrot*
*1 onion*
*2½ cups water*
*1 chicken bouillon cube*
*2 tbsps butter or margarine*
*2 tbsps flour*
*Pinch of grated nutmeg*
*1 tsp basil*
*Salt*
*Pepper*

GARNISH

*Chopped parsley*

### METHOD

Peel and finely dice the onion and carrot. Cut tomatoes into quarters and squeeze out seeds into a strainer. Strain seeds and retain the juice. Melt the butter in a pan. Fry the onion and carrot gently until the onion is transparent. Draw off heat and stir in the flour, nutmeg and basil. Add tomatoes, juice and water, return to heat and stir until boiling. Add crumbled chicken bouillon cube and salt and pepper to taste. Cover and simmer for 30 minutes. Push the soup through a strainer and return to pan. Adjust seasoning and reheat. Garnish with chopped parsley.

## SHRIMP PASTRY PUFFS

Wonderfully enticing is the only way to describe these delicate puffs. You will be amazed how quickly they disappear from the buffet table.

Preparation Time: 15 minutes
Cooking Time: 25-30 minutes
Oven Temperature: 400°F
Serves: 4

### INGREDIENTS

CHOUX PASTRY

½ cup flour
⅓ cup butter
½ cup water
2-3 eggs
Salt

FILLING

1¼ cups milk
2½ tbsps butter
2½ tbsps flour
2 tbsps white wine
¾ cup shrimp
2 hard-cooked eggs, quartered
Nutmeg
1 bay leaf
1 tsp chopped dill
Salt
Pepper

### METHOD

Prepare the pastry. Sift flour with a pinch of salt. Place butter and water in a pan over a gentle heat. When butter is melted, bring water to the boil. Take off the heat and immediately tip in all the flour. Beat until the mixture is smooth and leaves the sides of the pan. Leave to cool. Whisk the eggs lightly and add by degrees to the mixture, beating thoroughly between each addition. (This part of the recipe may be done with an electric mixer or in a food processor.) When finished, the paste should be smooth and shiny and hold its shape when dropped from a spoon. Lightly grease a baking sheet and sprinkle it lightly with water. Place the pastry mixture by heaped teaspoonfuls onto the sheet. If desired, the puffs can be made slightly larger by using a tablespoon. Bake until the puffs are firm to the touch and a good golden brown. For the sauce, melt the butter over a gentle heat and blend in the flour. Stir in the milk gradually and add the bay leaf. Add the wine and bring the mixture to the boil, stirring constantly. Remove the bay leaf, add the shrimp, dill and eggs, and adjust the seasoning. Cut the pastry puffs almost in half through the middle and fill with the shrimp and egg mixture. Serve hot or cold.

Facing page: the tiled cupolas of the church of Atrani, perched on the rocky south coast of the Sorrento peninsula.

Traditional village life continues in many of the Sorrento-peninsula villages untouched by tourism.

## STUFFED EGGS

Eggs are important in a balanced diet, but are often thought boring. A creative filling soon makes them much more enticing.

Preparation Time: 20 minutes
Cooking Time: 15 minutes
Serves: 4

### INGREDIENTS

*6 medium eggs*
*1 tbsp vinegar*
*1 small can of pink salmon*
*Paprika*
*2 tbsps peas*
*4-5 mushrooms*
*1 8oz package cream cheese*
*Salt*
*Pepper*

### GARNISH

*Stuffed olive*
*Red pepper or tomato*
*Black olive*

### METHOD

Put eggs into a saucepan of gently boiling water with 1 tbsp of vinegar and boil gently for 12 minutes. Remove and rinse immediately in cold water. Remove shells carefully and keep eggs in cold water until ready for use. Cut boiled eggs in half and carefully remove yolks. Rinse whites. Push yolks through a sieve and put aside for fillings. Soften cream cheese by beating. Drain and flake salmon. Mix carefully with one-third cream cheese. Add a pinch of paprika and salt and pepper to taste. Pipe or spoon filling into 4 egg whites. Garnish with half a stuffed olive. Wash and trim mushrooms. Chop very finely and add to one-third of cream cheese. Add salt or pepper to taste. Pipe or spoon filling into 4 egg whites. Garnish with red pepper or tomato. Cook peas until tender. Push through a strainer. Add yolks of eggs and one-third cream cheese. Pipe or spoon filling into remaining 4 egg whites and garnish with a slice of black olive.

# VEGETABLE SOUP

Tomato paste gives this soup its vibrant color.

Preparation Time: 20 minutes
Cooking Time: 50 minutes
Serves: 4

## INGREDIENTS

*2 medium onions, peeled and finely chopped*
*1 carrot, finely diced*
*½ small turnip, finely diced*
*2¾ cups beef stock*
*2 tbsps butter or margarine*
*1 leek, cut into small rings*
*1 tbsp tomato paste*
*2 tbsps chopped parsley*
*Salt*
*Pepper*

GARNISH

*Chopped parsley*

## METHOD

Melt the butter in a saucepan and add onions. Cook gently over a low heat for 5 minutes or until transparent. Add carrot and turnip, stock, seasoning and parsley. Bring to the boil and simmer gently for 15 minutes. Add leek and tomato paste and simmer for a further 20 minutes. Garnish with chopped parsley. Serve hot.

# ORANGE, GRAPEFRUIT AND MINT SALAD

Refreshing and light, this is the ideal summer appetizer.

Preparation Time: 20 minutes, plus chilling time
Serves: 4

## INGREDIENTS

*2 grapefruit*
*3 oranges*
*1 tbsp sugar*
*4 sprigs of mint*

GARNISH

*Mint sprig*

## METHOD

Cut the peel and pith off the grapefruit and oranges. Cut carefully inside the skin of each segment to remove each section of flesh. When skin only is left, squeeze to extract juices over a pan. Repeat with all the fruit. Add sugar to pan and set over a gentle heat until sugar dissolves and cool. Meanwhile, alternate the orange and grapefruit segments in a dish. Chop mint finely and add to fruit syrup. Carefully spoon syrup over fruit. Chill. Garnish with a sprig of mint.

Previous pages: the Gulf of Salerno seen from the gardens of the Palazzo Rufolo in Ravello. Right: the Bridge of Sighs, which links the Doge's Palace with the Pozzi Prison, in Venice.

## SHELL PASTA WITH TARAMASALATA

This attractive appetizer has an unusual appearance and a mouthwatering flavor.

Preparation Time: 15 minutes
Cooking Time: 15 minutes
Serves: 4

### INGREDIENTS

*1  9oz package shell pasta*
*1 cup taramasalata*
*2 tbsps lemon juice*
*10 black olives, pips removed, and chopped*
*1 tbsp black caviar or lumpfish roe*

### TO MAKE TARAMASALATA

*½ cup smoked salmon roe*
*Half an onion, grated*
*8 slices white bread, crusts removed*
*4 tbsps milk*
*⅓ cup olive oil*
*2 tsps lemon juice*
*Black pepper*

### METHOD

Crumble the bread into a bowl and add milk. Set aside to soak. Scoop the salmon roe out of its skin, and break it down with a wooden spoon. Squeeze the bread dry in a strainer. Add onion and bread to salmon roe, and mix well. Add oil and lemon juice very gradually, alternating between the two. Beat until smooth and creamy. Add pepper to taste, and salt if necessary. Cook pasta shells in lots of boiling salted water for 10 minutes or until *al dente*. Rinse in hot water, and drain well. Sprinkle with lemon juice; toss together with taramasalata, and garnish with caviar and black olives. Serve immediately.

# CHEESE PUFFS

These tasty little cheese-filled puffs are suitable as a
snack or party treat.

Preparation Time: 20 minutes
Cooking Time: 20 minutes
Serves: 4

## INGREDIENTS

### DOUGH

*1 cup flour*
*Pinch of salt*
*⅓ cup butter or margarine*
*1 cup water*
*3 medium eggs, lightly beaten*

### FILLING

*½ cup Fontina cheese, grated*
*½ cup Parmesan cheese, grated*
*1 egg, beaten*
*1 egg yolk, beaten, for glaze*

## METHOD

Pre-set oven to 375°F. Sift the flour and salt onto a sheet of
wax paper. Place butter and water in pan over gentle heat.
When butter has melted, bring to boil and immediately add
all the flour. Beat well until mixture is smooth. Leave to
cool. Add eggs gradually to mixture, beating well. Using a
teaspoon or a pastry bag with a plain tube, shape mixture
into balls about the size of golf balls onto a lightly greased
baking sheet. Place in oven and increase heat to 400°F.
Bake for 10 minutes until firm on outside. Remove from
oven and make a hole in bottom or side. Mix together
cheese and egg. Pipe in cheese mixture and brush tops with
egg yolk. Return to oven for 5 minutes. Serve immediately.

## STUFFED MUSHROOMS

Stuffed vegetables are always a popular choice as an appetizer. Mushrooms in particular are enhanced by the flavor of the stuffing.

Preparation Time: 15 minutes
Cooking Time: 20 minutes
Oven Temperature: 400°F
Serves: 4

### INGREDIENTS

4 large or 8 medium mushrooms, stalks discarded
1 tbsp olive oil
2 medium onions, peeled and chopped finely
8oz spinach, trimmed, cooked and chopped finely
2 tbsps fresh white breadcrumbs
4 tbsps butter or margarine
4 cloves garlic, minced
1 egg, beaten
½ tsp nutmeg
Salt
Pepper

GARNISH

1 tbsp chopped parsley

### METHOD

Heat the butter in pan. Add garlic, onion and nutmeg and fry gently until onion has softened. Remove from pan and set aside to cool. Meanwhile, heat oil in pan and sauté mushrooms on both sides until lightly browned. Place underside-up in a shallow ovenproof dish. Mix together onion mixture, spinach, breadcrumbs, and salt and freshly ground black pepper to taste. Stir in beaten egg. Cover each mushroom cap with the mixture, shaping neatly. Cover with aluminum foil and bake in a hot oven for 10 minutes. Serve immediately, garnished with chopped parsley.

The world-famous fourteen-foot tilt of the Tower of Pisa.

The Corinthian columns of the Temple of Vespasian and the well-preserved Ionic Temple of Saturn, both part of the Forum, in ancient Rome.

## ANCHOVY PÂTÉ WITH CRUDITÉS

The cheese used in this recipe is soft and creamy, with a lovely delicate flavor.

Preparation Time: 15 minutes
Serves: 4

### INGREDIENTS

*8oz canned anchovies*
*¼ cup olive oil*
*2oz Bel Paese*
*½ cup pitted black olives*
*2 tbsps capers*
*1 tbsp Dijon mustard*
*1 tsp ground pepper*

### METHOD

Put all the ingredients into the bowl of a blender or food processor and run the machine until well mixed. The mixture may have to be worked in two batches. Serve with Italian bread or toast, and raw vegetables of all kinds – tomatoes, mushrooms, celery, radishes, green beans, cauliflower, carrots, cucumber, peppers, green onions, or quarters of hard-cooked eggs.

## MELON AND PROSCIUTTO

This favorite Italian appetizer is simple to make yet absolutely delicious for any occasion.

Preparation Time: 20 minutes
Serves: 4

### INGREDIENTS

*1 large ripe melon*
*16 thin slices prosciutto ham*

### METHOD

Cut the melon in half lengthwise, scoop out the seeds and discard them. Cut the melon into quarters and carefully pare off the rind. Cut each quarter into four slices. Wrap each slice of melon in a slice of prosciutto and place on a serving dish. Alternatively, place the melon slices on the dish and cover with the slices of prosciutto, leaving the ends of the melon showing. Serve immediately.

## MUSSEL SOUP

Mussel soup always looks impressive; the taste is wonderful too, when garlic is used to enhance the flavor.

Preparation Time: 15 minutes
Cooking Time: 20 minutes
Serves: 4

### INGREDIENTS

*2 quarts live mussels, scrubbed clean*
*2 onions, peeled and chopped*
*2 cloves garlic, minced*
*2 tbsps chopped parsley*
*2 tbsps butter or margarine*
*1¼ cups dry white wine*
*2 tbsps lemon juice*
*Salt*
*Pepper*

GARNISH

*Chopped parsley*

### METHOD

Place mussels, butter, garlic, onions, wine, parsley and a pinch of freshly ground black pepper in a pan. Place over a high heat, cover and cook for a few minutes. Shake the pan to move the mussels and distribute the heat well. When mussels have all opened, transfer to serving dish and keep warm. Discard any that remain closed. Strain juices and return to pan. Reduce liquid by half over a high heat. Adjust seasoning. Whisk in lemon juice and pour hot soup over mussels. Serve immediately, sprinkled with chopped parsley.

The church of San Frediano in Cestello.

## STUFFED PEPPERS

It is important to ensure that the peppers are properly cooked as some people find it difficult to eat a whole one when it is still crispy.

Preparation Time: 30 minutes
Cooking Time: 30-40 minutes
Oven Temperature: 375°F
Serves: 6

### INGREDIENTS

*6 even sized peppers (green or red)*
*¼ cup oil*
*1 medium onion, peeled and chopped*
*2 cloves garlic, peeled and chopped*
*2 tomatoes, chopped*
*1 green chili, chopped*
*1 cup plain boiled rice*
*1 medium potato, peeled and diced*
*½ tsp salt*
*¾ tsp freshly ground black pepper*
*½ cup shelled peas*
*1¼ tbsps lemon juice*
*1¼ tbsps chopped parsley or coriander leaves*
*2½ tbsps beef stock or water*

### METHOD

Cut a slice from the top of each pepper; scoop out the center seeds. Heat the oil and fry the onion for 1-2 minutes. Add the garlic, tomatoes and green chili and stir-fry for 2-3 minutes. Add the rice, potato, salt and pepper, peas and lemon juice and parsley. Cover and cook for 2-4 minutes. Arrange the peppers in an ovenproof dish and stuff the peppers with the rice mixture. Pour the stock around the peppers. Bake for 20-30 minutes, basting occasionally with the juices. Serve hot.

## GOURMET MUSHROOMS

This impressive appetizer is suitable for any dinner party, no matter how daunting the guest list may be.

Preparation Time: 20 minutes
Cooking Time: 15 minutes
Serves: 4-6

### INGREDIENTS

*¾lb cultivated mushrooms*
*3 artichoke hearts, thinly sliced*
*Juice of 1 lemon*
*1 white celery heart, cut into strips*
*½lb shrimps, cooked, shelled and deveined*
*16 asparagus tips, cooked and drained*
*¾ cup mayonnaise*
*2 tbsps olive oil*
*2 ripe tomatoes, peeled and pressed through a sieve*
*Salt*

### METHOD

Peel mushroom caps, simmer for 15 minutes in water to cover. Drain them well. Sprinkle artichoke hearts with half the lemon juice to keep them from darkening. Put mushrooms, topped with artichokes, celery, shrimp and asparagus in little piles in a large glass bowl. Chill. Mix mayonnaise with oil, remaining lemon juice and tomato pulp. Add salt to taste. Serve this sauce with vegetables.

## MINESTRONE

Every generation loves this classic Italian soup. In this recipe, potatoes replace the pasta to make the perfect winter appetizer.

Preparation Time: 20 minutes plus overnight soaking
Cooking Time: 2 hours
Serves: 8-10

### INGREDIENTS

*8oz dried white cannellini beans*
*2 tbsps olive oil*
*1 large ham bone, preferably prosciutto*
*1 onion, chopped*
*2 cloves garlic, crushed*
*4 sticks celery, sliced*
*2 carrots, diced*
*1 small head Savoy cabbage or 1lb fresh spinach, well washed*
*4oz green beans, cut into 1 inch lengths*
*8oz tomatoes, peeled, seeded and diced*
*1 dried red chili pepper*
*10 cups water (or half beef stock)*
*Salt and pepper*
*1 sprig fresh rosemary*
*1 bay leaf*
*3 potatoes, peeled and cut into small dice*
*3 zucchini, trimmed and cut into small dice*
*1 tbsp chopped fresh basil*
*1 tbsp chopped fresh parsley*
*Grated Parmesan cheese*
*Salt and pepper*

### METHOD

Place the beans in a large bowl, cover with cold water and leave to soak overnight. Heat the oil in a large stock pot and add ham bone, onion and garlic. Cook until onion has softened but not colored. Add the celery, carrots, cabbage and green beans. If using spinach, reserve until later. Drain the beans and add them to the pot with the tomatoes and the chili pepper. Add the water and bring to the boil, skimming the surface as necessary. Add the rosemary and bay leaf and simmer, uncovered, until the beans are tender, about 1¼ hours. Add the potatoes and cook for the further 20 minutes. Add the zucchini and spinach and cook, skimming the surface, about 20 minutes longer. Remove the ham bone, rosemary and bay leaf and add basil and parsley. Serve with Parmesan cheese.

The restored thirteenth-century castle of the Scalingers in Sirmione, Lake Garda.

The extensive harbor of Messina, in Sicily, where modern buildings now surround the old.

## CHILLED SHRIMP, AVOCADO AND CUCUMBER SOUP

Cold soups are a delight during the summer, particularly when they include such delicious ingredients.

Preparation Time: 15 minutes
Cooking Time: 15 minutes
Serves: 4

### INGREDIENTS

*8oz unpeeled shrimp*
*1 large, ripe avocado*
*1 small cucumber*
*1 small bunch dill*
*Juice of half a lemon*
*1¼ cups chicken stock*
*2½ cups plain yogurt*
*Salt and pepper*

### METHOD

Peel all the shrimp, reserving shells. Add shells to the chicken stock and bring to the boil. Allow to simmer for about 15 minutes. Cool and strain. Peel the avocado and cut it into pieces. Cut 8 thin slices from the cucumber and peel the rest. Remove seeds and chop the cucumber roughly. Put avocado and cucumber into a food processor or blender and process until smooth. Add a squeeze of lemon juice, and strain on the cold chicken stock. Reserve a sprig of dill for garnish, and add the rest to the mixture in the processor and blend again. Add about 2 cups of yogurt to the processor and blend until smooth. Add salt and pepper. Stir in peeled shrimp by hand, reserving a few as garnish. Chill soup well. Serve in individual bowls, garnished with a spoonful of yogurt, a sprig of dill, and thinly sliced rounds of cucumber.

# MUSSELS ALLA GENOVESE

Attractive and impressive, this succulent appetizer is sure to please all your guests.

Preparation Time: 15 minutes
Cooking Time: 5-8 minutes
Serves: 4

## INGREDIENTS

1 quart mussels
Lemon juice
1 shallot, finely chopped
1 handful fresh basil leaves
1 small bunch parsley
4-5 walnut halves
1 clove garlic
2 tbsps freshly grated Parmesan cheese
3-6 tbsps olive oil
2 tbsps butter
Salt and pepper
Flour or oatmeal

GARNISH

*Fresh bay leaves or basil leaves*

## METHOD

Scrub the mussels well and discard any with broken shells. Put mussels into a bowl of clean water with a handful of flour or oatmeal. Leave for ½ hour, then rinse under clear water. Chop shallot finely and put into a large saucepan with lemon juice. Cook until shallot softens. Add mussels and a pinch of salt and pepper. Cover the pan and cook the mussels quickly, shaking the pan. When mussel shells have opened, take mussels out of the pan, set aside and keep warm. Strain the cooking liquid for possible use later. To prepare Genovese sauce, wash the basil leaves and parsley, peel the garlic clove and chop roughly, and chop the walnuts roughly. Put the herbs, garlic, nuts, 1 tbsp grated cheese and salt and pepper into a food processor and work to chop roughly. Add butter and work again. Turn machine on and add oil gradually through the feed tube. If the sauce is still too thick, add the reserved liquid from cooking the mussels. Remove top shells from mussels and discard. Arrange mussels evenly in 4 shallow dishes, spoon some of the sauce into each, and sprinkle the top lightly with remaining Parmesan cheese. Garnish with bay or basil leaves and serve.

## SOLE SURPRISE

These little puff paste pockets filled with spinach and sole make an interesting luncheon or appetizer.

Preparation Time: 30 minutes
Cooking Time: 30 minutes
Oven Temperature: 425°F
Serves: 4

### INGREDIENTS

*4 small or 2 large fillets of sole*
*8oz frozen puff paste*
*8oz frozen spinach*
*¼ cup butter*

SAUCE

*2 tbsps butter*
*2 tbsps flour*
*1 cup milk*
*Pinch fennel*
*Salt and pepper*
*½ cup grated cheese*

### METHOD

Roll out the defrosted paste into a rectangle 5 × 8 inches. Cut it down the center in both directions to make four rectangles 2½ × 4 inches. Carry out the following procedure with each one. Fold over, short sides together. Cut out the center with a sharp knife, leaving ½ inch all round. Roll out the centerpiece on a floured board until it is the same size as the ½ inch "frame". Brush the edges with milk and put the "frame" on the base. Brush the top with milk and put them on a greased baking sheet. Bake them in the oven, 425°F, for 10-15 minutes. Meanwhile, put the spinach in a pan with ¼ inch water and a little salt. Cover and cook for 4-5 minutes. Drain and beat in half the butter. Skin the fillets and, if necessary, cut them in two. Use the rest of the butter to coat two plates and put the fillets on one and cover them with the other. Cool them over a pan of boiling water for twenty minutes. For the sauce, melt 2 tbsps butter with the flour to make a roux. Gradually stir in the milk. Bring to the boil. Reduce the heat and add fennel and salt and pepper; cook for another minute or two. Remove from the heat and stir in the grated cheese. Divide the spinach between the four boxes. Lay the sole on top and coat with the cheese sauce.

The village of Rivello in the arid mountains above the Gulf of Policastro on the southwest coast.

The packed harbor at
Porto Sannazzaro,
Mergillina, Naples.

## OMELET SOUP

"Minestra di Frittata" is a deliciously different soup
which, once tried, is sure to become a family favorite.

Preparation Time: 5 minutes
Cooking Time: 10 minutes
Serves: 4

### INGREDIENTS

4 eggs
1 cup fresh white breadcrumbs
3 tbsps chopped parsley
1 tsp chopped marjoram
Salt and pepper
2 tbsps butter
6 cups chicken broth
Parmesan cheese to serve

### METHOD

Beat the eggs well and stir into them the breadcrumbs, 2
tbsps parsley and marjoram. Sprinkle with salt and pepper.
Heat the butter in a medium frying pan. Pour in enough egg
mixture to make a very thin omelet. As soon as it is golden
on one side, turn and cook on the other. Transfer to a plate.
Continue until all egg mixture has been used. In a large pan
bring the chicken broth to the boil. Season with salt and
pepper. While it is heating, roll each omelet up tightly. Cut
into very thin slices. When broth is boiling add the omelet
slices. Heat for 1-2 minutes. Serve with remaining parsley
and grated Parmesan cheese.

Facing page: one of the many small bridges which span the maze of canals in Venice. Overleaf: a Gothic-style church in the hills near Spoleto.

## LANGOUSTINE AND AVOCADO COCKTAIL

Langoustines were once plentiful in the bay of Naples. Unfortunately, today, it is often necessary to substitute shrimp.

Preparation Time: 20 minutes
Serves: 4

### INGREDIENTS

*8oz cooked langoustines or large shrimp*
*2 oranges*
*2 large, ripe avocados*
*1 small red onion or 2 green onions*
*¼ cup whipping cream*
*2 tbsps ketchup*
*2 tbsps mayonnaise*
*2 tsps lemon juice*
*12 (approx) black olives, pitted and sliced*
*2 tsps brandy*
*Pinch of Cayenne pepper*
*Pinch sugar*
*Salt*
*Freshly ground pepper*
*Lettuce*

### METHOD

Peel the oranges over a bowl to reserve juice. Peel the cooked langoustines and set aside. To prepare dressing, whip cream until thick, and mix with ketchup, mayonnaise, lemon juice, Cayenne, sugar, salt and pepper, brandy and some of the reserved orange juice to let down to the proper consistency – the dressing should be slightly thick. Chop onion finely. Cut avocados in half lengthwise and take out stones. Peel the avocados carefully and cut each half into 4-6 long slices. Shred the lettuce and put onto serving dishes. Arrange avocado slices in a fan shape on top of the lettuce. Brush each slice lightly with orange juice to keep green. Arrange an orange segment in between each slice. Pile langoustines up at the top of the avocado fan and coat with some of the dressing. Garnish with olives and sprinkle over chopped onion.

## GARLIC FRIED SCALLOPS

Two of Italy's favorite ingredients, garlic and seafood are brought together in this simple yet stylish dish.

Preparation Time: 10 minutes
Cooking Time: 6-8 minutes
Serves: 4

### INGREDIENTS

*16 scallops*
*1 large clove garlic, peeled and chopped finely*
*4 tbsps butter*
*3 tbsps chopped parsley*
*2 lemons*
*Seasoned flour*

### METHOD

Rinse scallops and remove black veins. If scallops are large, cut in half horizontally. Squeeze the juice from 1 lemon. Sprinkle scallops lightly with seasoned flour. Heat butter in a frying pan and add chopped garlic and scallops. Fry until pale golden brown. Pour over lemon juice, and cook to reduce the amount of liquid. Toss in the chopped parsley. Pile scallops into individual scallop shells or porcelain baking dishes. Keep warm, and garnish with lemon wedges before serving.

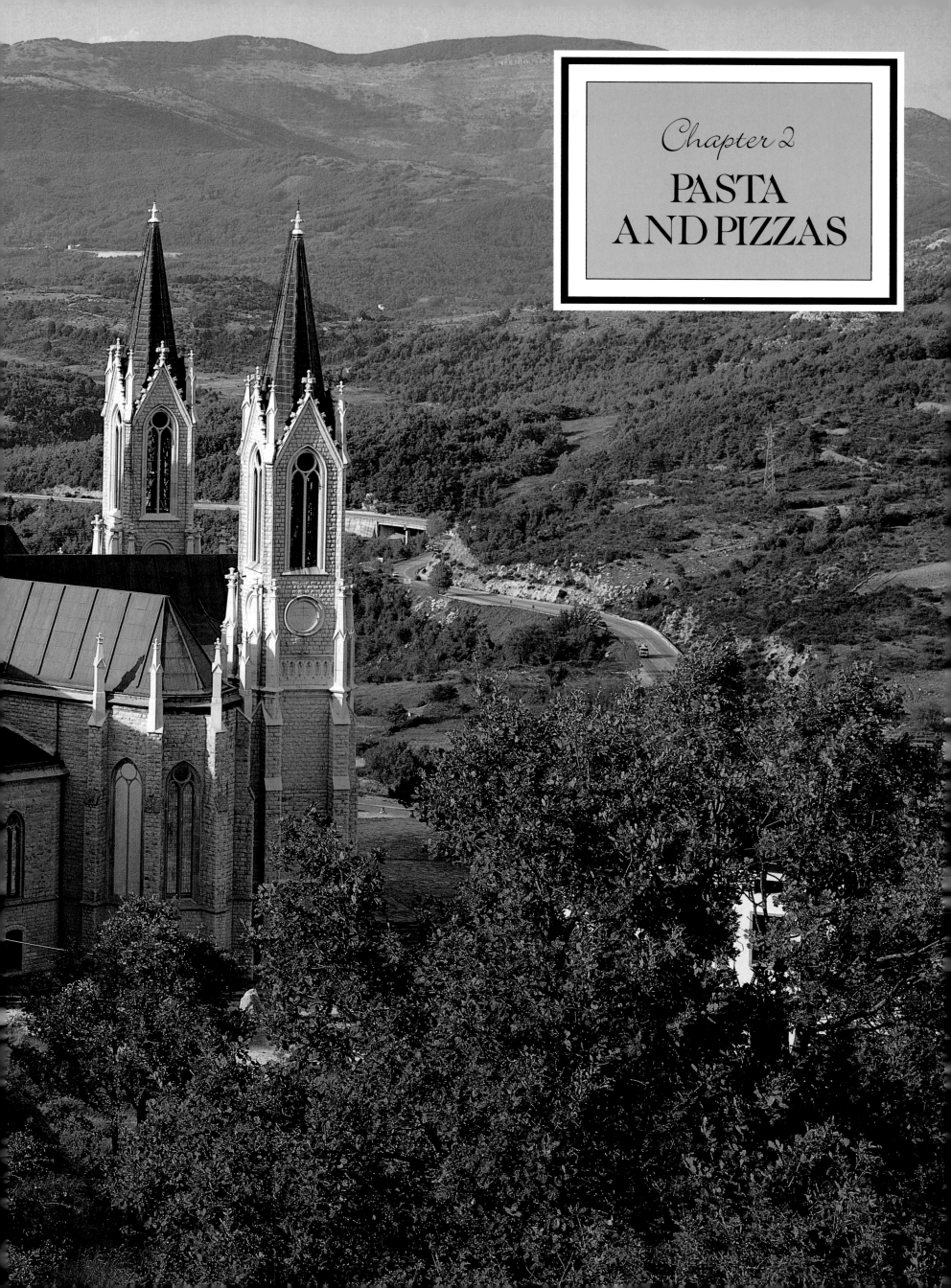

Right: the hilltop town of Trevi, in Umbria.

## MIXED VEGETABLE PIZZA TOPPING

Pizza toppings are, of course, one of the most adaptable features of Italian cooking. This one has a dazzling array of ingredients.

Preparation Time: 30 minutes
Cooking Time: 20 minutes
Oven Temperature: 450°F
Serves: 4-6

### INGREDIENTS

2½ tbsps olive oil
1 small onion, peeled and chopped
2 scallions, chopped
1 medium zucchini, trimmed and thinly sliced
4 mushrooms, sliced
Salt and freshly ground black pepper to taste
6-8 canned tomatoes, chopped
2 tsp tomato paste
8 pitted black olives
2 tomatoes, thinly sliced
1 green pepper, seeded and chopped
1 green chili, chopped
1¼ tsps dried oregano
1½ cups Mozzarella cheese, Cheddar cheese or a mixture of the two, cut into thin slivers
2½ tbsps grated Parmesan cheese

### METHOD

Heat the olive oil in a large frying pan, add the onions and sauté for 1-2 minutes. Add the zucchini and sauté for 2 minutes. Add the mushrooms and salt and pepper to taste and stir fry for 1 minute to glaze the vegetables. Remove from the heat and cool. Mix the chopped tomato with the tomato paste and spread evenly over the pizza base. Spoon the vegetable mixture over the pizza and arrange the olives, sliced tomatoes, green pepper and green chili on top. Sprinkle with the oregano, the slivers of cheese and the grated Parmesan cheese. Bake in oven for 12-15 minutes, or until the edge of the pizza is golden brown and crusty.

## NEAPOLITAN PIZZA

Naples provides the influence for this delicious pizza which is sheer perfection when served with a glass of Chianti.

Cooking Time: 30-40 minutes
Oven Temperature: 400°F
Serves: 4-6

### INGREDIENTS

Pizza dough made with 4½ cups all-purpose flour
2 cups chopped tomato pulp (skin and seeds removed) or 1 can peeled Italian tomatoes, drained, seeds removed and chopped
1lb Mozzarella cheese
1 can (2oz) anchovies or 4 salted anchovies
1 tsp crumbled oregano
¼ cup olive oil

### METHOD

On a greased baking sheet, stretch out dough large enough to make a 14-inch round. Pinch edge to make a rim. Cover with chopped tomato and slices of Mozzarella. Arrange anchovies like a lattice on top of cheese. Sprinkle on oregano and oil. Bake in a preheated oven for 30-40 minutes. Serve piping hot from the oven.

## PENNE WITH SPICY CHILI SAUCE

Italy meets Mexico in this Italian recipe with a difference. Red chilies add spice and complement the flavor of pasta and bacon.

Preparation Time: 15 minutes
Cooking Time: 40 minutes
Serves: 4

### INGREDIENTS

*1  9oz package penne*
*1 onion, peeled and chopped*
*1 large can (about 2 cups) plum tomatoes*
*2 red chili peppers, seeds removed, and chopped finely*
*2 cloves garlic, minced*
*1 tbsp olive oil*
*4 strips bacon, diced*
*¼ cup pecorino cheese, grated*

*2 green onions, chopped*
*Salt and pepper*

### GARNISH

*4 green onions (cut into 2 inch strips. Keeping one end intact, cut into strips. Soak in chilled water until the flower has opened)*

### METHOD

Chop tomatoes, removing seeds by straining juice. Heat oil in a pan, and fry garlic, onion and bacon gently for 10 minutes. Add tomato, chili peppers, chopped green onions, half the cheese, and salt and pepper to taste. Cook, uncovered, for 20 minutes. Ten minutes before sauce is ready, cook the penne in lots of boiling salted water for 10 minutes, or until tender but still firm. Rinse under hot water, and drain well. Put into a warmed serving dish, and toss together with half the sauce. Pour remaining sauce on top, and garnish with green onion flowers and remaining cheese if desired. Serve at once.

Facing page: the city of Florence seen from Piazzale Michelangelo.

### ITALIAN PASTA PIE

There is a delicious range of ingredients in this unusual
Italian pie.

Preparation Time: 35 minutes
Cooking Time: 1 hour 5 minutes
Oven Temperature: 375°F
Serves: 6-8

## INGREDIENTS

*1¼lbs puff paste*
*1lb fresh spinach, cooked and drained thoroughly*
*½ cup ricotta cheese*
*1 clove garlic, peeled and minced*
*Salt and freshly ground black pepper to taste*
*Generous pinch ground nutmeg*
*4oz pasta shapes, cooked until just tender*
*3oz shelled mussels*
*1 tbsp chopped fresh basil*
*1 egg, beaten*

TO GLAZE PASTRY

*Beaten egg*
*Grated Parmesan cheese*

## METHOD

Roll out ⅔ of the puff paste quite thinly and use to line the
sides and base of a loose-bottomed 7-inch round cake pan;
press the pastry carefully into the shape of the pan,
avoiding any cracks or splits. Roll out the remaining pastry
to a circle large enough to cover the top of the cake pan
generously. Mix the spinach with the ricotta cheese, garlic,
salt, pepper and nutmeg to taste, cooked pasta, mussels and
the beaten egg; spoon the filling into the pastry-lined pan.
Brush the rim of the pastry with beaten egg; lay the rolled-
out portion of pastry over the filling and press the adjoining
pastry edges together to seal. Trim off the excess pastry,
and pinch the edges decoratively. Cut decorative shapes
from the pastry trimmings and fix on top of the pie; glaze
with beaten egg and sprinkle with grated Parmesan cheese.
Bake in the oven for 45 minutes; cover with a piece of foil
and cook for a further 20 minutes. Unmold carefully from
the pan and serve the pie hot, cut into wedges. Note: the top
of the pie can be sprinkled with a few pine kernels prior to
baking, if liked.

The Sella Massif, one
of the Dolomite peaks
in northern Italy.

Facing page: the triumphal Arch of Constantine, built to mark his victory over Maxentius in A.D. 312.

## CANNELLONI WITH SPINACH AND RICOTTA

Cannelloni is made even more lively with the addition of spinach and ricotta cheese.

Preparation Time: 20 minutes
Cooking Time: 1 hour 20 minutes
Oven Temperature: 350°F
Serves: 4

### INGREDIENTS

*2½ tbsps olive oil or melted butter*
*1 large onion, peeled and finely chopped*
*2 large cloves garlic, peeled and minced*
*15oz can peeled tomatoes, chopped*
*1¼ tbsps tomato paste*
*Salt and freshly ground black pepper to taste*
*1¾ tsps dried basil*
*¾ tsp dried oregano*
*¾lb cannelloni tubes*
*5 tbsps thick spinach puree*
*½lb Ricotta cheese*
*2½ tbsps grated Parmesan cheese*

### METHOD

To make the sauce: heat the oil or butter and fry the onion and garlic for 2-3 minutes. Add the tomatoes and tomato paste and mix well. Simmer for 2 minutes. Add the salt and pepper, basil and oregano. Cover and simmer for 10-15 minutes until thick.

Bring a large pan of salted water to the boil; cook the cannelloni tubes for 10 minutes until just tender. Do not overboil. Lift out the cannelloni tubes and put them into a bowl of cold water to cool quickly. Drain well. Mix together the spinach, ricotta and salt and pepper to taste. Fill the cannelloni tubes with the spinach mixture and arrange them in a greased shallow ovenproof dish. Pour the tomato sauce over the cannelloni and sprinkle with the Parmesan cheese. Bake for 20-30 minutes or until the top is browned and bubbling. Serve at once.

A plethora of small yachts crowds the harbor at Rapallo.

## FARFALLE WITH TOMATO SAUCE

Farfalle or pasta bows look wonderfully appetizing served simply with a tomato sauce.

Preparation Time: 10 minutes
Cooking Time: 30 minutes
Serves: 4

### INGREDIENTS

*1  9oz package farfalle (pasta butterflies/bows)*
*4 small cans (about 4 cups) tomato sauce*
*1 tbsp olive oil*
*1 onion, peeled and sliced*
*2 cloves garlic, minced*
*½ tsp dry basil*
*Salt and pepper*
*2 tbsps chopped fresh basil or chopped parsley*
*Parmesan cheese, grated*

### METHOD

Heat the oil in a deep pan. Add garlic and onion, and cook until softened. Add dry basil, and cook for 30 seconds. Add tomato sauce and season with salt and pepper. Bring to the boil, reduce heat, and simmer, uncovered, for about 20 minutes, or until sauce is reduced by half and stir in the fresh parsley or basil. Meanwhile, cook the pasta in a large pan of boiling salted water until tender but still firm – about 10 minutes. Rinse in hot water, and drain well. Toss sauce through pasta. Serve with grated Parmesan cheese. Serve immediately.

## PASTA SHELLS WITH MUSHROOM SAUCE

The wonderful taste of mushrooms is used to greatest effect when combined solely with pasta.

Preparation Time: 5 minutes
Cooking Time: 15 minutes
Serves: 4

### INGREDIENTS

*1  9oz package pasta shells*
*8oz mushrooms*
*2 tbsps butter or margarine*
*1 tbsp flour*
*1 cup milk*
*Salt and pepper*

### METHOD

Rinse the mushrooms and chop them roughly. Melt butter in a saucepan and add mushrooms. Fry for 5 minutes, stirring occasionally. Stir in the flour and cook for 1 minute. Draw off the heat and add milk gradually, stirring continuously. Bring to the boil and cook for 3 minutes. Season with salt and pepper. Meanwhile, cook the pasta shells in lots of boiling salted water for 10 minutes, or until tender but still firm. Rinse in hot water and drain well. Place in a warmed serving dish, and pour over mushroom sauce. Serve immediately.

Santa Maria della Salute, built in the sixteenth-century in Venice as a symbol of hope following a year of plague.

## PIZZA MARINARA

Seafood pizzas are a popular choice in Italian restaurants, so why not surprise your friends by treating them to a home-made one instead.

Preparation Time: 15 minutes
Cooking Time: 25-30 minutes
Oven Temperature: 425°F
Serves: 4

### INGREDIENTS

*1 cup flour, sifted*
*1 tsp baking powder*
*½ tsp salt*
*⅓ cup milk*
*2 tbsps salad oil*
*½ cup canned tomatoes*
*1 tsp tomato paste*
*1 clove crushed garlic*
*½ tsp oregano*
*½ tsp basil*
*Fennel seeds*
*Salt*
*Pepper*
*¼ cup shrimp*
*4 anchovies*
*¼ cup clams*
*6-8 mussels*
*1 tsp capers*
*2-3 black olives*
*6 slices Mozzarella cheese*

### METHOD

Sift flour, baking powder and salt into a bowl and add milk and oil. Stir vigorously until mixture leaves the sides of the bowl. Press it into a ball and knead it in the bowl for about 2 minutes until smooth. Cover, and leave it to sit while preparing sauce. Put tomatoes, tomato paste, herbs, seasoning and garlic together in a small saucepan. Bring to the boil and reduce to thicken. Leave to cool. Roll out the pizza into a 12-inch circle. Spread the sauce evenly, leaving a ½-inch border around the edge. Scatter over the shell fish, anchovies, olives and capers. Place cheese slices on top of the fish. Bake in a pre-set oven until cheese browns lightly and the crust is crisp.

The Temple of Dioscuri, in Agrigento, on the island of Sicily.

## CRESPELLE ALLA BOLOGNESE

Pancakes are found in one form or another throughout the world. In this recipe Italian crespelles are complemented by a classic Bolognese filling.

Preparation Time: 45 minutes
Cooking Time: 1 hour 15 minutes
Oven Temperature: 400°F
Serves: 6-8

### INGREDIENTS

#### BOLOGNESE FILLING

*2 tbsps butter or margarine*
*1 tbsp olive oil*
*2 onions, finely chopped*
*8oz ground beef*
*1 small green pepper, seeded, cored and finely chopped*
*4oz canned plum tomatoes*
*1 tbsp tomato paste*
*½ cup beef stock*
*1 bay leaf*
*2 tsps chopped basil*
*1 tsp chopped oregano*
*2 tbsps sherry*
*Salt and Pepper*

#### CRESPELLE BATTER

*3 eggs*
*1 cup all-purpose flour*
*Pinch salt*
*1 cup water*
*2 tsps olive oil*
*Melted butter*

#### TOMATO SAUCE

*1 tbsp butter or margarine*
*1 clove garlic, minced*
*1 onion, finely chopped*
*1lb canned plum tomatoes*
*Salt, pepper and a pinch of sugar*
*Fresh basil leaves*

### METHOD

Heat the butter and oil in a deep saucepan for the Bolognese filling. Put in the onion and cook slowly until soft but not colored. Increase the heat and add the beef. Stir the beef while cooking, until all the meat is brown. Add chopped pepper, tomatoes and their juice, tomato paste, stock, herbs, salt and pepper to taste and simmer gently for about 45 minutes or until the mixture thickens, stirring occasionally. Add the sherry and cook for a further 5 minutes and set aside. Sift the flour for the crespelle with a pinch of salt. Break the eggs into a bowl and beat to mix thoroughly. Mix the flour into the eggs gradually, beating all the time until the mixture is smooth. Add water and the oil and stir in well. Cover the bowl with a damp cloth and leave in a cool place for 30 minutes. Heat the crêpe pan or a 7-inch frying pan. Lightly grease with the melted butter and pour a large spoonful of the batter into the center of the pan. Swirl the pan to coat the base evenly. Fry until the crespelle is brown on the underside, loosen the edge with a palette knife, turn over and brown the other side. Stack and wrap in a clean towel until needed.

To make the tomato sauce, melt the butter in a small saucepan and cook the garlic and onion slowly for about 5 minutes, or until softened but not colored. Reserve whole basil leaves for garnish and chop 2 tsps. Add the tomatoes to the onions and garlic along with the basil, salt, pepper and a pinch of sugar. Cook for about 10-15 minutes or until the onions are completely soft. Drain to remove the seeds, pressing the pulp against the strainer to extract as much liquid as possible. To assemble, lay the crespelle out on a large, clean work surface and put 2 heaped spoonfuls of Bolognese filling into each. Roll up and place in an ovenproof dish. Repeat until all the crespelle have been filled.

Put into oven and heat for about 8 minutes. Heat the tomato sauce and spoon over the crespelle before serving. Garnish with basil leaves and serve immediately.

# CANNELLONI

This favorite Italian dish is made easier by using ready-made cannelloni shells.

Preparation Time: 10 minutes
Cooking Time: 1 hour
Oven Temperature: 350°F
Serves: 4

## INGREDIENTS

*12 cannelloni shells*
*2 tbsps Parmesan cheese, grated*
*1 tbsp oil*

FILLING

*1lb ground beef*
*1 tbsp olive oil*
*1 onion, peeled and chopped*
*2 cloves garlic, minced*
*1 cup chopped, cooked spinach*
*½ tsp oregano*
*½ tsp basil*
*1 tsp tomato paste*
*4 tbsps cream*
*1 egg, lightly beaten*
*Salt and pepper to taste*

TOMATO SAUCE

*1 tbsp olive oil*
*1 onion, peeled and chopped*
*1 clove garlic, minced*
*2 small cans (about 2 cups) tomato sauce*
*2 tbsps tomato paste*
*Salt*
*Pepper*

BECHAMEL SAUCE

*1 slice of onion*
*3 peppercorns*
*1 small bay leaf*
*1 cup milk*
*2 tbsps butter or margarine*
*2 tbsps flour*
*Salt*
*Pepper*

## METHOD

### To make filling

Heat the oil in a pan, and fry garlic and onion gently until soft and transparent. Add meat and cook, stirring continuously, until well browned. Drain off any fat, add tomato paste, basil and oregano, and cook gently for 15 minutes. Add spinach, egg, cream, and salt and pepper to taste. Cook cannelloni in a large pan of boiling salted water for 15-20 minutes, until tender. Rinse in hot water and drain. Fill carefully with meat mixture, using a pastry bag with a wide, plain tube, or a teaspoon.

### To make tomato sauce

Heat oil in pan. Add onion and garlic, and cook gently until transparent. Add tomato sauce to the pan with tomato paste and salt and pepper to taste. Bring to boil, and then simmer for 5 minutes. Set aside.

### To make Béchamel sauce

Put milk in pan with onion, peppercorns and bay leaf. Heat gently for 1 minute, taking care not to boil, and set aside to cool for 5 minutes. Strain. Melt butter in pan. Remove from heat and stir in flour. Gradually add cool milk, and bring to boil, stirring continuously, until sauce thickens. Add seasoning.

Spread tomato sauce on the base of an ovenproof dish. Lay cannelloni on top, and cover with Béchamel sauce. Sprinkle with grated cheese, and bake in a moderate oven for 30 minutes. Serve immediately.

Above: the rocky coastline along the Gulf of Salerno. Overleaf: the picturesque fishing village of Atrani on the Amalfi coast.

## MACARONI CHEESE WITH ANCHOVIES

Anchovies appear often in Italian cooking and are used in an enormous range of dishes.

Preparation Time: 5 minutes
Cooking Time: 15 minutes
Serves: 4

### INGREDIENTS

*1  9oz package macaroni*
*4 tbsps butter or margarine*
*3 tbsps flour*
*2 cups milk*
*½ tsp dry mustard*
*¾ cup Fontina cheese, grated*
*6-8 anchovy fillets*
*Salt*
*Pepper*

### METHOD

Drain anchovies, and set enough aside to slice to make a thin lattice over the dish. Chop the rest finely. Cook the macaroni in plenty of boiling salted water for 10 minutes, or until tender but still firm. Rinse in hot water and drain well. Meanwhile, melt the butter in a pan. Stir in the flour and cook for 1 minute. Remove from heat, and gradually stir in the milk. Return to heat and bring to the boil. Simmer for 3 minutes, stirring continuously. Stir in the mustard, anchovies, and half the cheese. Season with salt and pepper to taste. Stir in the macaroni, and pour into an ovenproof dish. Sprinkle the remaining cheese over the top, and make a latticework with the remaining anchovies. Brown under a hot broiler. Serve immediately.

The Temple of Genii Augusti, in Pompeii.

## PENNE WITH HAM AND ASPARAGUS

Ham and asparagus make a delightful combination when mixed with penne. The shape of this pasta is described by the Italian word penne, which means quills.

Preparation Time: 20 minutes
Cooking Time: 8 minutes for the sauce
10-12 minutes for the pasta
Serves: 4

### INGREDIENTS

*8oz penne*
*12oz fresh asparagus*
*4oz cooked ham*
*2 tbsps butter or margarine*
*1 cup heavy cream*

### METHOD

Using a swivel vegetable peeler, scrape the sides of the asparagus spears, starting about 2 inches from the top. Cut off the ends of the spears about 1 inch from the bottom. Cut the ham into strips about ½ inch thick. Bring a sauté pan of water to the boil, adding a pinch of salt. Move the pan so it is half on and half off direct heat. Place in the asparagus spears so that the tips are off the heat. Cover the pan and bring back to the boil. Cook the asparagus spears for about 2 minutes. Drain and allow to cool. Cut the asparagus into 1-inch lengths, leaving the tips whole. Melt the butter in the sauté pan and add the asparagus and ham. Cook briefly to evaporate the liquid, and add the cream. Bring to the boil and cook for about 5 minutes to thicken the cream. Meanwhile, cook the pasta in boiling salted water with 1 tbsp oil for about 10-12 minutes. Drain the pasta and rinse under hot water. Toss in a colander to drain and mix with the sauce. Serve with grated Parmesan cheese, if desired.

Siena's magnificent cathedral was begun in 1229, but not completed until 1380.

## SPAGHETTI WITH TOMATO, SALAMI AND GREEN OLIVES

Salami and spaghetti is an unusual combination which brings home the versatility and fun of Italian cooking.

Preparation Time: 15 minutes
Cooking Time: 15 minutes
Serves: 4

### INGREDIENTS

*1  9oz package spaghetti*
*2 small cans (about 2 cups) tomato sauce*
*5oz salami, sliced and shredded*
*1 cup green olives, pitted and chopped*
*1 clove garlic, minced*
*2 tbsps olive oil*
*½ tbsp oregano*
*¼ cup pecorino cheese, grated*
*Salt and pepper*

### METHOD

Combine tomato sauce, oregano, salami and olives in a saucepan and heat gently. Add salt and pepper to taste. Meanwhile, cook spaghetti in plenty of boiling salted water for 10 minutes, or until tender but still firm. Drain well. Heat olive oil and freshly-ground black pepper in the pan used to cook the spaghetti. Add spaghetti, and pour the sauce over. Toss well. Serve immediately with pecorino cheese.

## PASTA WITH TOMATO AND YOGURT SAUCE

Tomato and yogurt sauce may sound unusual, but the taste is simply delicious.

Preparation Time: 5 minutes
Cooking Time: 40  minutes
Serves: 3-4

### INGREDIENTS

*1  9oz box pasta shells*
*⅓ cup plain yogurt*
*1 tbsp butter or margarine*
*1 tbsp flour*
*½ cup beef stock*
*2 small cans tomato sauce*
*1 bay leaf*
*Sprig of thyme*
*Parsley stalks*
*Salt and pepper*

### METHOD

Melt butter in a pan. Stir in the flour, and pour in the stock gradually. Add tomato sauce, bay leaf, thyme and parsley stalks. Season with salt and pepper. Bring to the boil and simmer for 30 minutes. Adjust seasoning. Meanwhile, cook pasta in plenty of boiling salted water for 10 minutes, or until tender but still firm. Rinse in hot water and drain well. Place in warmed serving dish; pour over tomato sauce, then yogurt. (Yogurt may be marbled through tomato sauce.) Serve immediately.

## MACARONI CHEESE WITH FRANKFURTERS

Children in particular will love the combination of macaroni cheese and sausages in this dish. Serve it any time for a hearty family meal.

Preparation Time: 10 minutes
Cooking Time: 20 minutes
Serves: 4

### INGREDIENTS

*1 9oz package macaroni*
*4 tbsps butter or margarine*
*3 tbsps flour*
*2 cups milk*
*1 tsp dried mustard*
*⅓ cup Cheddar cheese, grated*
*8 Frankfurters*
*Salt*
*Pepper*

GARNISH

*1 pimento, cut into strips*

### METHOD

Poach the Frankfurters for 5-8 minutes. Remove skins and, when cold, cut into diagonal slices. Cook macaroni in plenty of boiling salted water for about 10 minutes, or until tender but still firm. Rinse in hot water and drain well.

Meanwhile, melt the butter in a pan. Stir in the flour, and cook for 1 minute. Draw off heat, and gradually add milk, stirring all the time. Bring to the boil, stirring continuously, and cook for 3 minutes. Add Frankfurters, grated cheese, mustard and salt and pepper to taste. Stir well. Add macaroni, and mix in well. Pour mixture into an oven-proof dish, and sprinkle the remaining cheese over the top. Make a lattice of pimento, and cook under a preheated broiler until golden brown. Serve immediately.

## PASTA AL FORNO

This quintessentially Italian dish will be requested time and time again.

Preparation Time: 10 minutes
Cooking Time: 1 hour
Oven Temperature: 375°F
Serves: 4

### INGREDIENTS

*1 9oz package macaroni*
*4 tbsps butter or margarine*
*¼ cup Parmesan cheese, grated*
*Pinch of grated nutmeg*
*2 eggs, beaten*
*1 medium onion, peeled and chopped*
*1 clove garlic, minced*
*1lb ground beef*
*2 tbsps tomato paste*
*¼ cup red wine*
*½ cup beef stock*
*2 tbsps chopped parsley*
*2 tbsps plain flour*
*½ cup milk*
*Salt*
*Pepper*

### METHOD

Set oven. Cook macaroni in plenty of boiling salted water for 10 minutes, or until tender but still firm. Rinse under hot water. Drain. Put one-third of the butter in the pan and return macaroni to it. Add half the cheese, nutmeg, and salt and pepper to taste. Leave to cool. Mix in half the beaten egg, and put aside. Melt half of the remaining butter in a pan, and fry onion and garlic gently until onion is soft. Increase temperature and add meat, and fry until browned. Add tomato paste, stock, parsley and wine, and season with salt and pepper. Simmer for 20 minutes. In a small pan, melt the rest of the butter. Stir in the flour and cook for 30 seconds. Remove from heat, and stir in milk. Bring to boil, stirring continuously, until the sauce thickens. Beat in the remaining egg and season to taste. Spoon half the macaroni into a serving dish and cover with the meat sauce. Put on another layer of macaroni and smooth over. Pour over white sauce, and sprinkle with remaining cheese, and bake in the oven for 30 minutes until golden brown. Serve immediately.

The village of Positano, on the Amalfi coast, now thrives on tourism rather than fishing.

Facing page: the brightly lit Rialto Bridge in Venice. Overleaf: Lago d'Idro in the Lombardy region.

## HARE SAUCE WITH WHOLE-WHEAT SPAGHETTI

This sophisticated dish illustrates the flexibility of Italian cooking. Any ingredient can be substituted for the more common, as long as it tastes good.

Preparation Time: 10 minutes
Cooking Time: 1 hour 15 minutes
Serves: 4

### INGREDIENTS

*1lb whole-wheat spaghetti*
*½lb hare or rabbit cut into small pieces*
*¼lb bacon, diced*
*2 onions, peeled and sliced*
*1 clove garlic, minced*
*2 tbsps olive oil*
*½ tsp oregano*
*1 tbsp flour*
*½ cup red wine*

### METHOD

Heat oil in heavy pan. Lightly brown hare pieces. Remove hare pieces and put aside. Add onion, bacon, garlic and oregano to oil, and fry until lightly colored. Draw off heat, and stir in flour with a metal spoon. Return to heat and cook for 2 minutes. Remove from heat, add wine, and return to heat, stirring until boiling. Add hare, cover pan, and simmer gently for about 1 hour, until hare is tender. Add salt and pepper to taste. When sauce is ready, cook spaghetti in lots of boiling salted water for about 10 minutes, or until tender but still firm. Rinse in hot water, and drain. Serve with hare sauce on top. Serve immediately.

### SPAGHETTI NEAPOLITANA

This quick, tasty meal is an ideal choice for midweek, when time is short and everyone is in a hurry.

Preparation Time: 5 minutes
Cooking Time: 30 minutes
Serves: 4

#### INGREDIENTS

*1lb spaghetti*
*2 small cans (about 2 cups) tomato sauce*
*2 tbsps olive oil*
*½ tsp oregano or marjoram*
*Salt*
*Pepper*
*2 tbsps chopped parsley*
*Parmesan cheese, grated*

#### METHOD

Heat oil in pan. Add oregano or marjoram, and cook for 30 seconds. Add tomato sauce, and salt and pepper. Bring to boil; reduce heat; simmer uncovered for 20-30 minutes. Meanwhile, cook spaghetti in lots of boiling salted water for about 10 minutes, or until tender but still firm. Rinse under hot water, and drain well. Pour tomato sauce over spaghetti, and toss gently. Sprinkle parsley over the top. Serve with Parmesan cheese. Serve immediately.

## *ITALIAN CASSEROLE*

The tastiest of Italian ingredients combine in this colorful
and hearty dish.

Preparation Time: 15 minutes
Cooking Time: 40 minutes
Oven Temperature: 350°F
Serves: 4

### INGREDIENTS

*1 cup small macaroni*
*2 tbsps butter or margarine*
*1 clove garlic, minced*
*1 onion, peeled and chopped*
*1 large can (about 2 cups) plum tomatoes*
*1 tbsp tomato paste*
*1 sweet red pepper, cored, seeds removed,
and chopped roughly*

*1 green pepper, cored, seeds removed,
and chopped roughly*
*10 black olives, halved, and stones removed*
*¼lb Mozzarella cheese, sliced thinly*
*½lb salami, cut into chunks*
*Salt*
*Pepper*

### METHOD

Cook the macaroni in plenty of boiling salted water for 10
minutes, or until tender but still firm. Rinse under hot water
and drain well. Place in a shallow, ovenproof dish.
Meanwhile, heat butter in pan, and fry onion and garlic
gently until soft. Add undrained tomatoes, tomato paste,
red and green peppers, salami and olives, and stir well.
Simmer uncovered for 5 minutes. Season with salt and
pepper. Pour over the macaroni, stir, and cover with the
sliced cheese. Bake uncovered in a moderate oven for 20
minutes, until cheese has melted. Serve immediately.

Facing page: the world-
famous Trevi Fountain
in Rome.

The breathtaking view from Mount Solaro towards Faraglioni, on Capri.

# BAKED CAPONATA AND NOODLES

Eggplant, green noodles and peppers are the main ingredients in this tasty dish, which has been popular in Italy for many years.

Preparation Time: 25-30 minutes
Cooking Time: 35-40 minutes
Oven Temperature: 375°F
Serves: 4

## INGREDIENTS

*1 medium onion, thinly sliced*
*2 tbsps olive oil*
*2 cloves garlic, peeled and finely chopped*
*1 large green pepper, seeded and cut into cubes*
*1 large red pepper, seeded and cut into cubes*
*1 medium eggplant, cubed*
*6 tomatoes, skinned, seeded and chopped*
*1 tbsp tomato paste*
*3 tbsps red wine*
*Salt and freshly ground black pepper to taste*
*½ cup green noodles, cooked*
*¾ cup grated cheese*

## METHOD

Fry the onion gently in the olive oil for 4 minutes; add the garlic, red and green peppers, eggplant and chopped tomatoes and cook, covered, for 5 minutes. Add the tomato paste, wine and salt and pepper to taste; simmer gently for 10-15 minutes, until the vegetables are almost soft. Remove from the heat and stir in the cooked noodles. Spoon into a shallow flameproof dish and sprinkle with the grated cheese. Bake in the oven for 15 minutes (alternatively, the dish can be flashed under a preheated broiler).

## LASAGNE NEAPOLETANA

This wonderfully colorful lasagne has long been a favorite in Naples, where it was invented.

Preparation Time: 25 minutes
Cooking Time: 1-1¼ hours
Oven Temperature: 375°F
Serves: 6

### INGREDIENTS

*9 sheets spinach lasagne pasta*

TOMATO SAUCE

*3 tbsps olive oil*
*2 cloves garlic, minced*
*2lbs fresh tomatoes, peeled, or canned tomatoes, drained*
*2 tbsps chopped fresh basil, six whole leaves reserved*
*Salt and Pepper*
*Pinch sugar*

CHEESE FILLING

*1lb ricotta cheese*
*4 tbsps unsalted butter*
*2 cups Mozzarella cheese, grated*

*Salt and Pepper*
*Pinch nutmeg*

### METHOD

Cook the pasta for 8 minutes in boiling salted water with 1 tbsp oil. Drain and rinse under hot water and place in a single layer on a damp cloth. Cover with another damp cloth and set aside. To prepare the sauce, cook the garlic in remaining oil for about 1 minute in a large saucepan. When pale brown, add the tomatoes, basil, salt, pepper and sugar. If using fresh tomatoes, drop into boiling water for 6-8 seconds. Transfer to cold water and leave to cool completely. This will make the peel easier to remove. Lower the heat under the saucepan and simmer the sauce for 35 minutes. Add more seasoning or sugar to taste. Beat the ricotta cheese and butter together until creamy and stir into the remaining ingredients. To assemble the lasagne, oil a rectangular baking dish and place 3 sheets of lasagne on the base. Cover with one third of the sauce and carefully spread on a layer of cheese. Place another 3 layers of pasta over the cheese and cover with another third of the sauce. Add the remaining cheese filling and cover with the remaining pasta. Spoon the remaining sauce on top. Cover with foil and bake for 20 minutes. Uncover and cook for 10 minutes longer. Garnish with the reserved leaves and leave to stand 10-15 minutes before serving

### *TORTIGLIONI ALLA PUTTANESCA*

This quick and easy pasta dish clearly shows that good cooking does not have to be complicated or expensive.

Preparation Time: 10 minutes
Cooking Time: 15 minutes
Serves: 4

### INGREDIENTS

1   9oz package tortiglioni, spiral pasta
1 small can (about 1 cup) plum tomatoes, drained
6-8 anchovy fillets
2 tbsps olive oil
2 cloves garlic, minced
½ tsp basil
Pinch chili powder
½ cup black olives, pitted and chopped
2 tbsps chopped parsley
Salt
Pepper

### METHOD

Chop tomatoes, remove seeds, and chop anchovies. Cook pasta in plenty of boiling salted water for 10 minutes, or until tender but still firm. Rinse in hot water, and drain. Pour into a warmed bowl. Meanwhile, heat oil in pan, add garlic, chili powder and basil, and cook for 1 minute. Add tomatoes, parsley, olives and anchovies, and cook for a few minutes. Season with salt and pepper. Pour sauce over pasta, and mix together thoroughly. Serve immediately.

Left: the harbor and medieval castle in the old Pisan village of Lerici.

## PASTA SPIRALS WITH CREAMY PARSLEY SAUCE

Pasta is so filling that it only needs a simple sauce to turn it into the perfect quick meal.

Preparation Time: 5 minutes
Cooking Time: 15 minutes

### INGREDIENTS

1  9oz package pasta spirals
2 tbsps butter or margarine
1 tbsp flour
1 cup milk
1 tbsp chopped parsley
1 tbsp lemon juice, or 1 tsp vinegar

### METHOD

Heat butter in pan; when melted, stir in flour. Cook for 1 minute. Remove from heat, and gradually stir in milk. Return to heat, and stir continuously until boiling. Cook for 2 minutes. Meanwhile, cook pasta spirals in lots of boiling salted water for 10 minutes, or until tender but still firm. Rinse in hot water, and drain well. Just before serving, add lemon juice and parsley to sauce, and pour over pasta. Serve immediately.

Alpine slopes near
Breuil Cervinia.
Overleaf: the drama of
St Peter's Church in
Rome by night.

## SPAGHETTI AMATRICIANA

Red chili pepper adds spice to this classic Italian dish.

Preparation Time: 10 minutes
Cooking Time: 20 minutes
Serves: 4

### INGREDIENTS

1  9oz package spaghetti
1 onion, peeled and chopped finely
6 slices bacon, cut into strips
1 large can (about 2 cups) plum tomatoes, drained, seeds
removed, and chopped roughly
1 red chili pepper, seeds removed, and chopped finely
2 tbsps olive oil
¼ cup pecorino cheese, grated

### METHOD

Heat oil in pan. Add onion and bacon, and cook over gentle heat until onion is soft but not colored. Drain off surplus fat. Add tomato and chili. Stir. Simmer gently for 5 minutes, stirring occasionally. Meanwhile, cook spaghetti in lots of boiling salted water for about 10 minutes, or until tender but still firm. Drain and return to pan. Add sauce and stir through. Serve with grated pecorino cheese.

## MEAT RAVIOLI

It is certainly not a case of familiarity breeding contempt with this Italian classic, it is as popular today as it has always been.

Preparation Time: 30 minutes
Cooking Time: 30 minutes
Serves: 4

### INGREDIENTS

#### DOUGH

*1¼ cups of bread flour*
*Pinch of salt*
*3 eggs*

#### FILLING

*4 tbsps butter or margarine*
*½lb ground beef*
*½ cup cooked spinach, chopped*
*2 tbsps breadcrumbs*
*2 eggs, beaten*
*½ cup red wine*
*1 onion, peeled and grated*
*1 clove garlic, minced*
*Salt*
*Pepper*

#### SAUCE

*1 small can (about 1 cup) plum tomatoes*
*1 small onion, peeled and grated*
*1 small carrot, diced finely*
*1 bay leaf*
*3 parsley stalks*
*Salt*
*Pepper*
*Parmesan cheese, grated*

### METHOD

#### To make filling

Heat butter in pan. Add garlic and onion, and fry gently for 1 minute. Add ground beef, and fry until browned. Add red wine, and salt and pepper to taste, and cook uncovered for 15 minutes. Strain juices and reserve them for sauce. Allow to cool. Add breadcrumbs, chopped spinach, and beaten eggs to bind. Adjust salt and pepper to taste.

#### To make dough

Sift flour in a bowl. Make a well in the center and add the eggs. Work flour and eggs together with a spoon, then knead by hand, until a smooth dough is formed. Leave dough to rest for 15 minutes. Lightly flour board, and roll out dough thinly into a rectangle. Cut dough in half. Shape the filling into small balls, and set them about 1½ inches apart on one half of the dough. Place the other half on top, and cut with a ravioli cutter or small pastry cutter. Seal the edges. Cook in batches in a large, wide pan with plenty of boiling salted water until tender – about 8 minutes. Remove carefully with a perforated spoon. Meanwhile, make sauce.

#### To make sauce

Put all ingredients in a saucepan. Add juice from cooked meat, and bring to boil. Simmer for 10 minutes. Strain, and return smooth sauce to pan. Adjust seasoning.

Put ravioli in a warm dish and cover with tomato sauce. Serve immediately, with grated Parmesan cheese.

A Doric temple on the Acropolis at Selinunte, in Sicily.

## SPAGHETTI WITH SWEETBREAD CARBONARA

Sweetbread recipes are always rare, and this one is particularly different with its unusual mixture of ingredients.

Preparation Time: 10-15 minutes
Cooking Time: 10 minutes
Serves: 4

### INGREDIENTS

*1 onion, chopped*
*3 tbsps olive oil*
*12oz whole-wheat spaghetti*
*Salt and freshly ground black pepper to taste*
*8oz calves' sweetbreads, blanched, skinned and chopped*
*6 tbsps dry white wine*
*4 eggs*
*¼ cup grated Parmesan cheese*
*2 tbsps chopped fresh basil*
*1 clove garlic, peeled and minced*

### METHOD

Fry the onion gently in the olive oil for 5 minutes. Meanwhile, cook the spaghetti in a large pan of boiling, salted water for about 10 minutes, until just tender. Add the chopped sweetbreads to the onion and fry gently for 4 minutes. Add the white wine and cook briskly until it has almost evaporated. Beat the eggs with the Parmesan cheese, basil, garlic, and salt and pepper to taste. Drain the hot, cooked spaghetti thoroughly, and immediately stir in the beaten egg mixture and the sweetbreads, so that the heat from the spaghetti cooks the egg. Garnish with basil and serve immediately.

Left: the octagon-shaped dome of the Cathedral of Santa Maria del Fiore in Florence was the masterpiece of the fifteenth-century architect Filippo Brunelleschi.

# PIZZA WITH PEPPERS, OLIVES & ANCHOVIES

The Italian pizza has become a favorite everywhere, probably because it is so adaptable. Here you can use our topping or include some of your own favorite ingredients.

Preparation Time: 40 minutes
Cooking Time: 10-15 minutes for sauce, 15 minutes for pizza
Oven Temperature: 400°F
Serves: 4

## INGREDIENTS

### PIZZA DOUGH

*½oz fresh yeast*
*½ tsp sugar*
*¾ cup lukewarm water*
*2 cups all-purpose flour*
*Pinch salt*
*2 tbsps oil*

### TOPPING

*2 tsps olive oil*
*1 onion, finely chopped*
*1 clove garlic, minced*
*1lb canned tomatoes*
*1 tbsp tomato paste*
*½ tsp each oregano and basil*
*1 tsp sugar*
*Salt and pepper*
*½ red pepper*
*½ green pepper*
*½ cup black olives, pitted*
*2oz canned anchovies, drained*
*1 cup Mozzarella cheese, grated*
*2 tbsps grated Parmesan cheese*

## METHOD

Cream the yeast with the sugar in a small bowl, add the lukewarm water and leave to stand for 10 minutes to prove. Bubbles will appear on the surface when ready. Sift flour and salt into a bowl, make a well in the center and add the oil and the yeast mixture. Using a wooden spoon, beat the liquid in the center of the well, gradually incorporating the flour from the outside until it forms a firm dough. Turn the dough out onto a floured surface and knead for 10 minutes, or until the dough is smooth and elastic. Place in a lightly oiled bowl or in a large plastic bag, cover or tie the bag and leave to stand in a warm place for 30 minutes, or until the dough has doubled in bulk. Knock the dough back and knead it into a smooth ball. Flatten the dough and roll out into a circle on a floured surface. The circle should be about 10 inches in diameter. To prepare the topping, heat the oil in a heavy-based saucepan and add the onion and the garlic. Cook until the onion and garlic have softened but not colored. Add the tomatoes and their juice, tomato paste, herbs, sugar, salt and pepper. Bring the sauce to the boil and then allow to simmer, uncovered, to reduce. Stir the sauce occasionally to prevent sticking. When the sauce is thick and smooth, leave it to cool. Spread the cooled sauce over the pizza dough. Sprinkle half the cheese on top of the tomato sauce and then arrange the topping ingredients. Sprinkle with remaining cheese and bake in oven for 15-20 minutes, or until the cheese is melted and bubbling, and the crust is brown.

Tall, green-shuttered houses built into the steep slope at Riomaggiore, Liguria. Overleaf: the colorful harbor in the fishing village of Portovenere, also in Liguria.

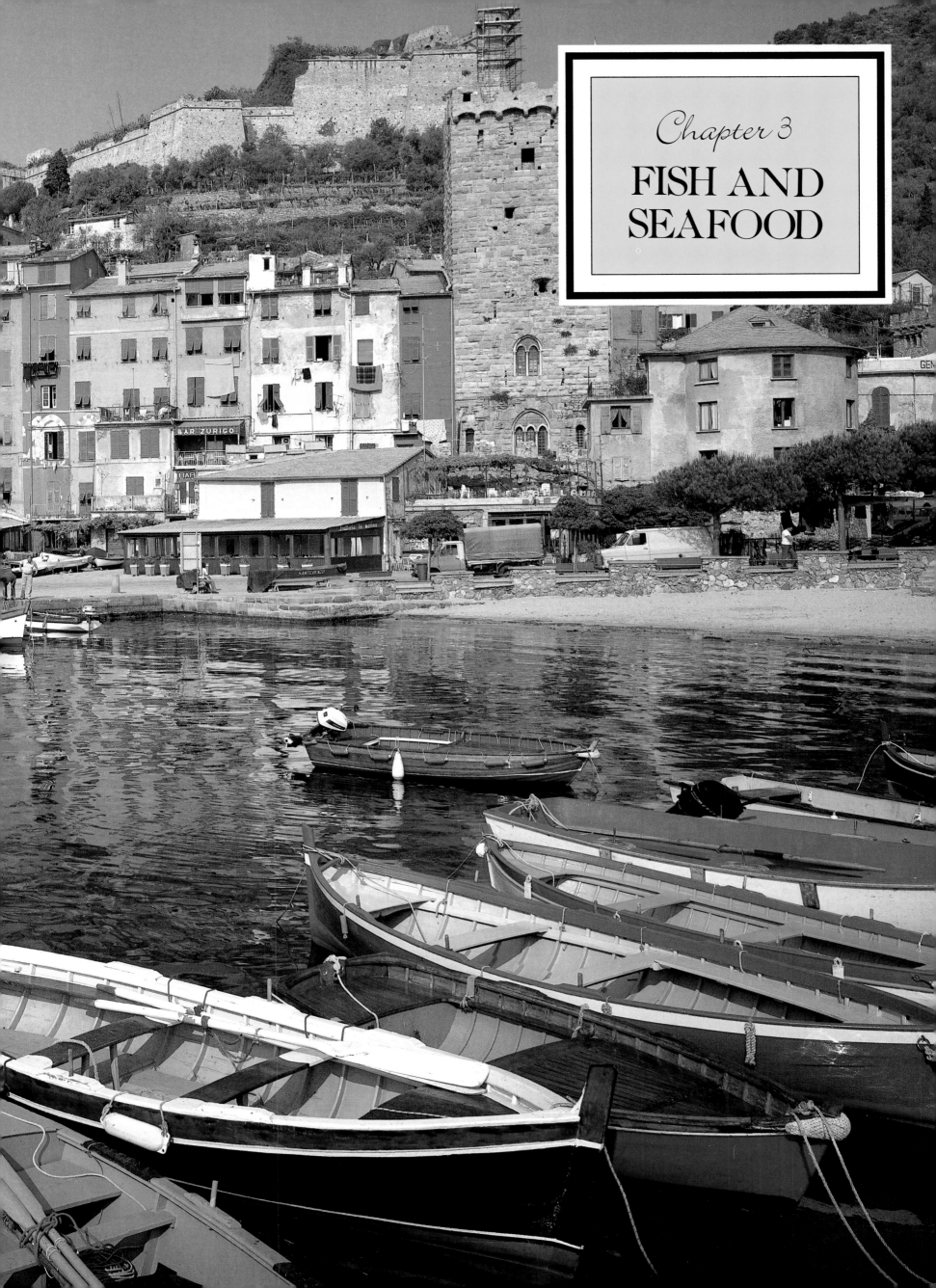

Chapter 3

# FISH AND SEAFOOD

## SHRIMP SALAD

Simple to prepare with a wonderful fresh flavor, this dish is a natural choice for a midweek treat.

Preparation Time: 10 minutes
Cooking Time: 15 minutes
Serves: 4

### INGREDIENTS

*3 cups pasta shells*
*8oz shrimp, shelled and deveined*
*½ cup mayonnaise*
*Juice of 1 lemon*
*Salt*
*Pepper*
*1 lettuce*
*1 cucumber, sliced*

### METHOD

Cook the pasta in plenty of boiling salted water for 10 minutes, or until tender. Drain, and rinse under cold water. Shake off excess water, put into a bowl, and pour over lemon juice. Leave to cool. Mix paprika into mayonnaise. Add shrimp to the mayonnaise, and toss. Arrange a bed of lettuce leaves and sliced cucumber in a dish, and pile pasta in center. Pile shrimp on top.

The Matterhorn, or Monte Cervino, which straddles the border between Switzerland and Italy.

## *TUNA AND FENNEL*

For this recipe, find the freshest tuna you can; combined with Florentine fennel it is simply delicious.

Preparation Time: 15 minutes
Cooking Time: 6-8 minutes
Serves: 4

### INGREDIENTS

*4 tuna steaks, cut (1 inch) thick*
*4 tbsps olive oil*
*4 tbsps white wine*
*Crushed black pepper*
*1 clove garlic*
*Salt*
*1 head Florentine fennel*

### METHOD

Peel garlic and cut into thin slivers. Push these into the tuna steaks with a sharp knife. Mix oil, wine and pepper and pour over steaks in a shallow dish. Leave to marinate in a refrigerator for 1 hour. Heat broiler to high and broil fish for 3-4 minutes per side, basting frequently with the marinade. Reserve the green, feathery tops of the fennel. Cut the head in half and slice into ¼ inch pieces. Put into boiling salted water and cook for 5 minutes. Season with salt and pepper and keep warm. Garnish the tuna steaks with reserved fennel top and serve with the cooked, sliced fennel.

## RED SNAPPER WITH HERB & MUSHROOM SAUCE

An unusual dish which is very Mediterranean in taste with its mixture of seafood, garlic and mushrooms.

Preparation Time: 30 minutes
Cooking Time: 20 minutes
Oven Temperature: 375°F
Serves: 4

### INGREDIENTS

*1lb small mushrooms, left whole*
*1 clove garlic, finely chopped*
*3 tbsps olive oil*
*Juice of 1 lemon*
*1 tbsp finely chopped parsley*
*2 tsps finely chopped basil*
*1 tsp finely chopped marjoram or sage*
*4 tbsps dry white wine mixed with ½ tsp cornstarch*
*Few drops anchovy paste*

*4 red snapper, each weighing about 8oz*
*2 tsps white breadcrumbs*
*2 tsps freshly grated Parmesan cheese*

### METHOD

Combine the mushrooms, garlic and olive oil in a small frying pan. Cook over moderate heat for about 1 minute, until the garlic and mushrooms are slightly softened. Add all the herbs, lemon juice and white wine and cornstarch mixture. Bring to the boil and cook until thickened. Add anchovy paste to taste. Set aside while preparing the fish. To clean the fish, cut along the stomach from the gills to the vent – the small hole near the tail. Clean out the cavity of the fish, leaving the liver, if desired. To remove the gills, lift the flap and snip them out with a sharp pair of scissors. Rinse the fish well and pat dry. Place the fish head to tail in a shallow ovenproof dish that can be used for serving. The fish should fit snugly into the dish. Pour the prepared sauce over the fish and sprinkle with the breadcrumbs and Parmesan cheese. Cover the dish loosely with foil and cook in the preheated oven for about 20 minutes. Uncover for the last 5 minutes, if desired, and raise the oven temperature slightly. This will lightly brown the fish.

One of the ten angels adorning the Ponte Sant'-Angelo in Rome.

The terracotta-colored rooftops of Florence.

## *DEVILED LOBSTER ITALIAN STYLE*

Lobster dishes are always special. This one makes a perfect celebration meal for two.

Preparation Time: 20 minutes
Cooking Time: 20-25 minutes
Oven Temperature: 375°F
Serves: 2

## INGREDIENTS

*2 live lobsters, about 1½lb each*
*3 tbsps butter*
*1 tbsp brown mustard*
*¼ cup brandy*
*Salt and pepper*
*2 tbsps olive oil*
*3 tbsps dry breadcrumbs*
*2 lemons sliced*

## METHOD

Drop lobsters into boiling salted water. When water re-boils, boil for 5 minutes. Drain and drench with cold water. Cut lobsters in half lengthwise, crack legs and claws. Remove ''sand sack'' and dark colored intestine. Reserve coral and tomalley. Mix butter until it is creamy. Stir in mustard and creamy parts of lobster after pressing them through a sieve. Light brandy in a cup and pour flaming liquid over mixture. When flames die, sprinkle with salt and pepper and mix thoroughly. Brush a baking dish with oil. Add lobster halves cut side up. Spread some of the mustard sauce over them. Bake in the preheated oven for about 15 minutes, basting from time to time with pan juices. Meanwhile, mix breadcrumbs with remaining mustard sauce. Remove pan from oven and spread the breadcrumb mixture over lobster halves. Bake for a further 5 minutes until well-browned. Place on a serving platter with shredded lettuce and lemon slices. Pour over pan juices and serve.

The Doge's Palace runs along one end of St Mark's Square, Venice.

## FISH MILANESE

Milan provides the influence for this delicious dish of fish coated in crispy crumbs and enlivened with the tang of lemon juice.

Preparation Time: 1 hour
Cooking Time: 6 minutes
Serves: 4

### INGREDIENTS

*8 sole or plaice fillets*
*2 tbsps dry vermouth*
*1 bay leaf*
*6 tbsps olive oil*
*Salt and pepper*
*Seasoned flour for dredging*
*2 eggs, lightly beaten*
*Dry breadcrumbs*
*Oil for shallow frying*
*6 tbsps butter*
*1 clove garlic, minced*
*2 tsps chopped parsley*
*2 tbsps capers*
*1 tsp chopped fresh oregano*
*Juice of 1 lemon*
*Salt and pepper*
*Lemon wedges and parsley to garnish*

### METHOD

Skin the fillets with a sharp filleting knife. Remove any small bones and place the fillets in a large, shallow dish. Combine the vermouth, oil and bay leaf in a small saucepan and heat gently. Allow to cool completely and pour over the fish. Leave the fish to marinate for about 1 hour, turning them occasionally. Remove the fish from the marinade and dredge lightly with the seasoned flour. Dip the fillets into the beaten eggs to coat, or use a pastry brush to brush the egg onto the fillets. Dip the egg-coated fillet into the breadcrumbs, pressing the crumbs on firmly. Heat the oil in a large frying pan. Add the fillets and cook slowly on both sides until golden brown. Cook for about 3 minutes on each side, remove and drain on paper towels. Pour the oil out of the frying pan and wipe it clean. Add the butter and the garlic and cook until both turn a light brown. Add the herbs, capers and lemon juice and pour immediately over the fish. Garnish with lemon wedges and sprigs of parsley.

## VERMICELLI PESCATORE

The exotic appearance of this seafood dish makes it the ideal choice for an impressive centerpiece.

Preparation Time: 15 minutes
Cooking Time: 40 minutes
Serves: 4

### INGREDIENTS

*¾ cup mussels*
*¾ cup clams*
*8oz cod fish fillets*
*4oz squid, cleaned*
*4 Gulf shrimp, cooked*
*4 fresh oysters, cooked*
*1 9oz package vermicelli*
*1 cup dry white wine*
*¼ cup olive oil*
*4 small cans (about 4 cups) tomato sauce*
*2 tbsps tomato paste*
*Half a green pepper, diced*

### METHOD

Prepare seafood. If using fresh mussels, clean closed mussels, removing beard, and cook in boiling water for 3 minutes until they open. (Discard any that remain closed.) Cool and remove from shells, keeping a few in shells for garnish if desired. Skin and bone the fillets, and cut fish into ½-inch pieces. Clean squid and cut into rings. Heat 2 tbsps oil in a pan, and add the squid. Fry gently until golden brown, then add wine, tomato, green pepper, and salt and pepper to taste. Simmer for 20 minutes then add fish. Simmer for a further 10 minutes, stirring occasionally. Add clams and mussels and, when mixture reboils, adjust seasoning. Meanwhile, cook spaghetti in lots of boiling salted water for 10 minutes, or until tender but still firm. Drain well. Add seafood, and toss. Garnish with shrimp and fresh oysters.

Wild flowers surround the Temple of Concord in Agrigento, Sicily.

This ancient villa in Ravello illustrates perfectly the architectural wealth which is so much a part of Italy's past.

## SEAFOOD PANCAKES

These are especially nice when made with sole and two or three scallops, but you can use 1½lb of any whitefish, filleted.

Preparation Time: Pancakes 1 hour 15 minutes, filling 15 minutes
Cooking Time: 45 minutes
Serves: 6

### INGREDIENTS

*12 thin pancakes*
*1½lb fish*
*4oz shrimp (cooked)*
*4oz mushrooms*
*1 tbsp butter*
*1 tbsp lemon juice in 2 fl oz water*
*1 medium onion*
*Bay leaf*
*6 peppercorns*
*1 tsp salt*
*⅓ cup butter*
*¾ cup flour*
*Glass white wine*
*2½ cups fish stock*
*Grated nutmeg*
*⅔ cup whipped cream*

### METHOD

Put washed fish trimmings in a pan with the bay leaf, peppercorns, salt and 2½ cups water. Bring to the boil and simmer for half an hour. Strain. Cut the sole, or other fish, diagonally into 1-inch strips and poach in the fish stock for 2 minutes. Remove the fish from the stock with a slotted spoon and set aside. Melt the tbsp of butter in a pan, add the mushrooms, sliced, the lemon juice and 4 tbsps of water, bring to the boil, reduce heat and cook for 1 minute. Remove mushrooms with a slotted spoon.

Melt ⅓ cup butter in a pan, stir in the flour and cook over a low heat for a minute or two. Add the white wine and bring to the boil. Remove the pan from the heat and slowly add the fish and mushroom stocks, stirring all the time. Return to the heat and simmer for 2 minutes. Season with salt and pepper and a little grated nutmeg. Remove from heat and stir in the whipped cream. Use half the sauce to mix in with the fish, shrimp and mushrooms. Divide this mixture between the 12 pancakes, rolling each one up and placing them, side by side, in a large, shallow, greased ovenproof dish. Pour over the rest of the sauce and heat through in the oven, 350°F, for about half an hour or until the top begins to brown. Allow 2 pancakes per person for a main course, or one each as a first course.

Fish and Seafood

# BAKED SEA BASS WITH FENNEL AND MIXED VEGETABLES

Fresh vegetables provide the perfect accompaniment to the delicate flavor of fresh fish.

Preparation Time: 30 minutes
Cooking Time: 35-40 minutes
Oven Temperature: 375°F
Serves: 4-6

## INGREDIENTS

*1 sea bass, about 2½lbs in weight, scaled, gutted and cleaned*
*Salt and freshly ground black pepper to taste*
*1 tbsp chopped fresh fennel*
*1 large clove garlic, peeled and finely chopped*
*Coarsely grated rind of ½ lemon*
*2 tbsps olive oil*
*4 tbsps dry white wine*

### MIXED VEGETABLES

*2 large carrots, peeled and cut into thin strips*
*3 stalks celery, cut into thin strips*
*4oz green beans*

### GARNISH

*Feathery sprigs of fennel or dill*

## METHOD

Season the sea bass inside and out; put the chopped fennel, garlic and lemon rind into the cavity of the fish. Lay the fish on a rectangle of greased foil, sitting on a cookie sheet; pinch up the edges of the foil. Brush the sea bass with olive oil and spoon over the dry white wine. Pinch the foil together over the fish to completely enclose it. Bake in the oven for 35-40 minutes (the foil can be folded back for the last 10 minutes cooking time, if liked). For the vegetables, steam over gently simmering water for about 10 minutes – they should still be slightly crunchy. Arrange the cooked sea bass on a large, oval serving platter and surround with small "bundles" of the steamed vegetables. Garnish with sprigs of fennel.

Ancient tombs in the necropolis, lying just outside the walls of Pompeii.

Right: the harbor of
Portofino in Liguria
plays host to the yachts
of rich visitors, as well
as to local fishing
boats.

## *SARDINE AND TOMATO GRATINÉE*

The nutritional value of oily fish is now widely
acknowledged, so be generous with the servings!

Preparation Time: 20-25 minutes
Cooking Time: 15 minutes
Oven Temperature: 425°F
Serves: 4

### INGREDIENTS

*2lbs large, fresh sardines*
*3 tbsps olive oil*
*⅔ cup dry white wine*
*8oz tomatoes*
*4 anchovies*
*2 tbsps dry breadcrumbs*
*¼ cup grated Parmesan cheese*
*2 tbsps chopped fresh herbs*
*2 leeks, cleaned and sliced*
*Salt and pepper*

### METHOD

Scale and clean the sardines. Heat oil in a large frying pan,
add the sardines and brown well on both sides. Remove
from the pan and set aside. Add leeks and cook slowly in
the oil from the sardines. When they are soft, pour in the
wine and boil to reduce by about two-thirds. Add tomatoes,
salt, pepper and herbs, and continue to simmer for 1
minute. Pour into an ovenproof dish and put the sardines on
top. Sprinkle with the cheese and breadcrumbs. Bake for
about 5 minutes. If desired, cut anchovy fillets lengthwise
into thinner strips and lay them on top of the gratinée
before serving.

The harbor of Portofino in Liguria plays host to the yachts of rich visitors, as well as to local fishing boats.

## FISHERMAN'S WHOLE-WHEAT PASTA SALAD

In the past fishermen used whatever happened to be in their nets. Luckily there are now fish shops to satisfy your needs.

Preparation Time: 20 minutes, plus cooling time
Cooking Time: about 10 minutes
Serves: 4

### INGREDIENTS

*3 cups whole-wheat pasta shapes (shells, wheels, etc.)*
*Salt and freshly ground black pepper to taste*
*4 tbsps olive oil*
*2 tbsps dry white wine*
*1 tbsp chopped parsley*
*3 green onions, chopped*
*½ cup shelled, cooked mussels*
*6 tbsps peeled shrimp*
*½ cup flaked crabmeat*
*12 black olives*

GARNISH

*Large peeled shrimp*

### METHOD

Cook the whole-wheat pasta in a large pan of boiling salted water until just tender – about 10 minutes. Meanwhile, prepare the dressing. Mix the olive oil with the white wine, parsley, and salt and pepper to taste. Drain the cooked pasta thoroughly and stir in the prepared dressing. Allow to cool. Mix in the chopped green onions and then carefully stir in the shell fish and add the black olives. Spoon into one large salad bowl, or four individual ones.

Facing page: a mountain river in Piedmont. Overleaf: the Punta della Dogana da Mar in Venice. The tower of the Customs House supports a gilded sphere symbolising fortune.

# SPAGHETTI MARINARA

Spaghetti and seafood is a classic Italian combination. This recipe is a perfect example of how it is too delicious to save only for special occasions.

Preparation Time: 10 minutes
Cooking Time: 20 minutes
Serves: 4

## INGREDIENTS

*1 9oz package spaghetti*
*1lb shrimp, shelled and deveined*
*8oz scallops, cleaned and sliced*
*6-8 anchovies*
*1 large can (about 2 cups) plum tomatoes, seeded and chopped*
*½ cup dry white wine*
*½ cup water*
*1 bay leaf*
*4 peppercorns*
*2 tbsps olive oil*
*1 tsp basil*
*2 cloves garlic, minced*
*1 tbsp tomato paste*
*1 tbsp chopped parsley*
*Salt and pepper*

## METHOD

Drain anchovies and cut into small pieces. Place water, wine, bay leaf and peppercorns in a pan. Heat to a slow boil. Add scallops and cook for 2 minutes. Remove and drain. Heat the oil, add garlic and basil, and cook for 30 seconds. Add tomatoes, anchovies and tomato paste. Stir until combined. Cook for 10 minutes. Meanwhile, cook the spaghetti in a large pan of boiling salted water for 10 minutes, or until tender but still firm. Drain. Add seafood to sauce, and cook a further 1 minute. Add parsley and stir through. Season with salt and pepper to taste. Toss gently. Pour sauce over spaghetti and serve immediately, sprinkled with parsley.

The port of Marina Grande on the island of Capri becomes crowded with tourists during the summer months.

## SHRIMP RISOTTO

Risotto enjoys widespread popularity and this recipe, with its blend of shrimp and Parmesan cheese, is especially appetizing.

Preparation Time: 15 minutes
Cooking Time: 25 minutes
Serves: 4

### INGREDIENTS

*1lb unpeeled shrimp*
*4 tomatoes*
*3 cloves garlic*
*1 large onion*
*3 tbsps olive oil*
*2 tbsps chopped parsley*
*1 glass white wine*
*1½ cups round Italian or risotto rice*
*1 tsp tomato paste*
*2 tbsps grated Parmesan cheese*
*Salt*
*Freshly ground pepper*

### METHOD

Skin, seed and chop tomatoes, and peel and chop garlic and onion. Peel shrimp, leaving 4 unpeeled for garnish. Cook wine and shrimp shells together and leave to cool. Heat olive oil in a fairly wide pan or sauté pan. Soften onion in the oil without browning. Add garlic and parsley. Fry gently for a minute. Add rice and strain on the wine. Add tomato paste and more water to just cover rice. Season with salt and pepper, stirring the rice, adding more water as it becomes absorbed. The rice will take about 20 minutes to cook. When it is cooked, toss in the peeled shrimp and cheese to heat through. Pile risotto into a serving dish and top with unpeeled shrimp. Sprinkle over some chopped parsley.

A cleric strolls under Bernini's colonnade, which encloses St Peter's Square in Rome.

## BUTTERED PERCH

The Italian love of seafood is clearly visible in this simple dish, which brings out all the flavor of the fish.

Preparation Time: 10 minutes
Cooking Time: 12-15 minutes
Serves: 4

### INGREDIENTS

*2lbs perch (or sole or other whitefish) fillets*
*½ cup butter*
*3 tbsps oil*
*Seasoned flour*
*2 eggs, beaten*
*Fine corn meal*
*Lemon juice*
*Salt*

### GARNISH

*Lemon wedges*
*Parsley sprigs*

### METHOD

Skin, wash and dry the fillets well, cut each lengthwise into 4 strips and toss in seasoned flour. Beat the eggs, adding a pinch of salt, then coat the fish before tossing it in the corn meal. Shake off the excess. Heat oil in a large frying pan and add 1 tbsp butter. Shallow-fry the fish briskly for about 5-6 minutes, frying in 2 or 3 batches. Drain on paper towels and keep warm. Melt remaining butter and add lemon juice. Pour over the fish and serve with lemon wedges and sprigs of parsley

The Elephant Fountain
and the cathedral in
Catania, Sicily.

## *SCAMPI FLORENTINE*

Colorful and tasty, this classic Italian dish has a texture
which is greatly enhanced by the addition of a cheese
topping.

Preparation Time: 15 minutes
Cooking Time: 15-20 minutes
Serves: 4

### INGREDIENTS

*1lb cooked scampi*
*2lbs fresh spinach*
*1 cup mushrooms*
*2 tomatoes, seeds removed*
*1 shallot*
*4 tbsps butter*
*1 tbsp flour*
*1¼ cups milk*
*½ cup grated Fontina cheese*

*Salt*
*Pepper*
*Nutmeg*

### METHOD

Rinse spinach well, removing any thick stalks, and put it
into a saucepan with a good pinch of salt. Cover and cook
for about 3-5 minutes. In a small saucepan, heat half of the
butter. Chop the shallot finely and cook it in the butter until
soft. Wipe and slice the mushrooms and cook with the
shallots. Drain the spinach well and chop finely. Mix the
shallots, mushrooms and tomatoes with the spinach, add
seasoning and a pinch of nutmeg, and put into an ovenproof
dish. Melt half the remaining butter in a saucepan and add
the flour. Gradually stir in the milk, return the sauce to the
heat and bring to the boil. Season with salt and pepper.
Grate the cheese and add half to the sauce. Shell scampi if
necessary. Heat remaining butter and quickly toss scampi
in it over heat. Put scampi on top of the spinach and cover
with sauce. Sprinkle remaining cheese over, and brown
quickly under a broiler. Serve immediately.

## SARDINES

Sardines are very common in Italian cuisine, where they are recognized as healthful as well as tasty.

Preparation Time: 20 minutes
Cooking Time: 25 minutes
Oven Temperature: 425°F
Serves: 4

### INGREDIENTS

*12 fresh or frozen sardines (or smelts)*
*½ cup mushrooms, chopped finely*
*2 shallots, peeled and chopped finely*
*2 cloves garlic, minced*
*2 tbsps butter or margarine*
*4 tbsps fresh breadcrumbs*
*1 tbsp lemon juice*
*2 tbsps chopped parsley*
*Pinch of freshly grated nutmeg*
*Salt*
*Pepper*

GARNISH

*Lemon slices*
*Cress*

### METHOD

Wash sardines or smelts and remove any scales. Cut along stomach, being careful not to cut through back. Remove head, gills and stomach sac. Remove backbone from head end to tail. Remove tail. Wash and pat dry with paper towels. Heat butter in pan. Add garlic, shallots and mushrooms and fry for 5 minutes. Remove from heat and add breadcrumbs, parsley, lemon juice, nutmeg and salt and pepper to taste. Spread sardine or smelt fillets with the stuffing and close up. Place in a greased baking pan. Bake in a hot oven for 15 minutes or until cooked. Garnish with lemon slices and cress, if desired, and serve hot or cold with buttered toast.

The skyline of Florence, seen from the cathedral.

# FRITTO MISTO MARE

These tasty seafood bites can be served as a dinner party appetizer, or with vegetables for a main meal.

Preparation Time: 10 minutes
Cooking Time: 5-6 minutes
Serves: 4

## INGREDIENTS

4-8 scallops
8oz uncooked shrimp
1lb whitebait, smelts or sprats, or whitefish such as sole or cod
½ pint shelled mussels
Vegetable oil for deep frying
Salt

### BATTER

1¼ cups water
2 tbsps olive oil
1 cup flour
1 tsp ground nutmeg
1 tsp ground oregano
Pinch salt
1 egg white

### GARNISH

Parsley sprigs
1 lemon

## METHOD

First make the batter so that it can rest for ½ hour while fish is being prepared. Blend oil with water, and gradually stir into flour sifted with a pinch of salt. Beat batter until quite smooth, and add the nutmeg and oregano. Just before using, fold in stiffly-beaten egg white. If using smelts or sprats, cut heads off the fish; if using whitefish, cut into chunks about 1 inch thick. Shell shrimp if necessary, If the scallops are large, cut them in half. Heat oil to 375°F. Dip fish and shellfish, one at a time, into batter, allowing surplus batter to drip off. Then put them into the frying basket and into the hot oil. Fry for 5-6 minutes, or until crisp and golden. Drain on crumpled paper towels. Sprinkle lightly with salt. Put fish on a heated dish and garnish with parsley sprigs and lemon wedges. If desired, a tartare sauce may be served.

# PASTA AND SMOKED SALMON

Whether plain or fancy, smoked salmon is superb. Tagliatelle brings out all the flavor of the salmon in this unusual dish.

Preparation Time: 10 minutes
Cooking Time: 18 minutes
Serves: 4

## INGREDIENTS

3oz plain tagliatelle or fettuccine
3oz whole-wheat tagliatelle or fettuccine
3oz spinach tagliatelle or fettuccine
8oz smoked salmon
¼ cup mushrooms
1 egg
⅔ cup heavy cream
1 tbsp chopped parsley
1 tsp chopped fresh basil
2 green onions, finely chopped
1 tbsp butter
1 jar red salmon caviar
Salt and pepper

## METHOD

Cook the pasta in boiling salted water until just tender. Drain under hot water and keep it warm. Slice and cook the mushrooms, with the onion, in the butter. Slice the smoked salmon into thin strips and set aside. Beat together the egg and heavy cream with the chopped herbs, salt and pepper. Add these to the onion and mushrooms, and heat through, stirring constantly. Do not allow mixture to boil. Toss with the pasta and the salmon. Top with red salmon caviar to serve.

Porto Sannazzaro at Mergillina, Naples.

# DEVILED STUFFED CRAB

Crab should always be bought as fresh as possible. If you can catch it yourself it will be all the more satisfying!

Preparation Time: 10-15 minutes
Cooking Time: 20 minutes
Oven Temperature: 375°F
Serves: 4

## INGREDIENTS

*2 cooked crabs*
*¼ cup shelled pistachio nuts*
*2 hard-cooked eggs*
*1 tbsp flour*
*1 tbsp butter*
*1¼ cups milk*
*1 green pepper*
*1 medium onion*
*2 tbsps chili sauce or hamburger relish*
*2 tsps white wine vinegar*
*2 tsps chopped dill pickles*
*1 tsp Dijon mustard*
*½ tsp Worcestershire sauce*
*Tabasco*
*3 tbsps butter or margarine*
*4 tbsps dry breadcrumbs*

*Chopped parsley*
*Salt*
*Pepper*

GARNISH

*Lemon wedges*
*Watercress*

## METHOD

Buy the crabs already cleaned, or if you wish to do it yourself, twist off all the legs, separate body from shell, and remove lungs and stomach. Cut body into 3 or 4 pieces with a sharp knife and pick out all the meat. Scrape brown meat from inside shell; crack large claws and remove meat, adding all this meat to the body meat. Crab shells may be washed and used to bake in. Prepare cream sauce. Melt 1 tbsp butter in a small saucepan. When foaming, take it off the heat and stir in flour, then the milk, gradually. Mix well. Return to heat and bring to boil, allowing it to thicken. Set aside to cool slightly. Chop the egg roughly, and cut the green pepper and onion into small dice. Break up crabmeat roughly. Chop pistachio nuts, and add all other ingredients to the white sauce. Lightly butter the clean shell or individual baking dishes. Fill with crabmeat mixture and top with dry crumbs. Melt 3 tbsps butter and sprinkle over the crumbs. Bake for 15 minutes, and brown under broiler if necessary. Sprinkle with chopped parsley and garnish with watercress and lemon wedges.

The gilded and enameled clock face of the Torre dell'Orologio in St Mark's Square, Venice.

## SEVICHE

Seviche is an imaginative and innovative way of using raw fish to create a health-conscious meal.

Preparation Time: 20 minutes
Serves: 4

### INGREDIENTS

*1lb codfish*
*⅔ cup lemon or lime juice*
*1 tbsp chopped shallot*
*1 green chili pepper*
*1 green pepper*
*2 tomatoes*
*1 tbsp chopped parsley*
*1 tbsp chopped fresh coriander*
*2 tbsps vegetable oil*
*1 small head iceberg lettuce*
*4 green onions*
*Salt*
*Pepper*

### METHOD

Skin cod and remove any bones. Wash and pat dry, then cut across grain into slices approximately ½ inch thick and 2½ inches long. Put into a bowl and pour over lime or lemon juice. Put in shallot. Slice chili pepper and remove the seeds, then chop finely and add it to the fish. Add seasoning and put into the refrigerator for 24 hours, well covered. Stir occasionally. When ready to serve, chop green onions and herbs. Slice pepper into short, thin strips. Plunge tomatoes into boiling water for about 4 seconds, then into cold water, and peel. Cut tomatoes in half, squeeze out the seeds, and slice into fine strips. Drain off lemon or lime juice from fish, and stir in oil. Add herbs, peppers and tomatoes, and toss. Spoon onto lettuce leaves in a serving dish and sprinkle over green onions.

Facing page: Clear blue seas and bright skies make the waters around Sorrento ideal for watersports.

St Peter's Square,
Vatican City, Rome

## CURRIED TUNA CANNELLONI

Don't allow the curry in this dish to put you off, it will
surprise and delight all pasta fanatics

Preparation Time: 15 minutes
Cooking Time: 45 minutes
Oven Temperature: 350°F
Serves: 4

### INGREDIENTS

*12 cannelloni shells*

#### FILLING

*2 tbsps butter or margarine*
*1 onion, peeled and chopped*
*1 stick of celery, chopped*
*½ cup mushrooms, cleaned and chopped*
*1 tbsp flour*
*1 tsp curry powder*
*½ cup milk*
*⅓ cup soured cream*
*⅓ cup mayonnaise*
*1 egg, lightly beaten*
*1  7oz can tuna fish*

*3 shallots, peeled and chopped*
*Salt*
*Pepper*

#### TOPPING

*4 tbsps breadcrumbs*
*¼ cup Cheddar cheese, grated*
*2 tbsps butter or margarine*

### METHOD

Cook cannelloni shells in a large pan of boiling salted
water for 15-20 minutes until tender. Rinse in hot water and
drain well. Meanwhile, melt butter in saucepan and fry
onion until transparent, add mushrooms and celery, and fry
for 5 minutes. Add curry powder and flour, and fry until
light golden brown. Draw off the heat, and gradually add
milk, stirring continuously. Return to heat and bring to the
boil. Cook for 3 minutes, stirring all the time. Add soured
cream, mayonnaise, and undrained flaked tuna. Season
with salt and pepper and stir until sauce boils. Simmer for 3
minutes. Add shallots and egg, and mix well. Spoon
mixture into cannelloni shells, and place in an ovenproof
dish. Sprinkle over a mixture of breadcrumbs and cheese,
and dot with butter or margarine. Bake in a moderate oven
for 20 minutes. Serve immediately.

The steep streets of
Capri Town on the
island of Capri.

## GREEN BEANS, HAZELNUTS AND LANGOUSTINES

Strange as this mixture may seem, the end result is mouthwatering.

Preparation Time: 15 minutes
Cooking Time: 20 minutes
Oven Temperature: 350°F
Serves: 4

### INGREDIENTS

*1lb green beans, trimmed*
*¾lb cooked langoustines or large shrimp*
*¼ cup whole hazelnuts, skinned*
*1 red pepper, stem and seeds removed, and sliced thinly*
*⅓ cup olive oil*
*3 tbsps white wine vinegar*
*1 tsp Dijon mustard*
*1 tbsp chopped parsley*
*1 small head iceberg lettuce, shredded*
*Salt*
*Pepper*

### METHOD

Toast hazelnuts in moderate oven for about 15 minutes or until golden brown. Allow to cool. Chop roughly. Bring salted water to the boil in a saucepan, and cook beans in it for about 4-6 minutes – they should remain crisp. Drain, refresh under cold water, drain again and dry. Cook pepper slices in boiling water for about 1 minute. Drain and refresh under cold water, and allow to dry. Whisk oil, vinegar, Dijon mustard and seasonings together. Peel langoustines, and mix together with beans, pepper, hazelnuts and dressing. Arrange lettuce on individual serving dishes, and pile remaining ingredients on top. Sprinkle parsley over the top to serve.

## EGG AND FISH FLAN

Fish and eggs make a healthful and hearty combination which will satisfy the biggest appetite.

Preparation Time: 30 minutes
Cooking Time: 45 minutes
Oven Temperature: 375°F
Serves: 6

### INGREDIENTS

DOUGH

*1 cup flour*
*Pinch of salt*
*1/3 cup butter or margarine*
*1 tbsp lard*
*Cold water*

FILLING

*2 eggs, beaten*
*8oz whitefish fillets*
*6-8 anchovies, drained*
*10 black olives, halved and stones removed*
*2 tbsps light cream*
*1 tbsp lemon juice*
*1 bay leaf*
*6 peppercorns*
*Parsley stalks*
*Slice of onion*
*1¼ cups cold water*
*1 onion peeled and chopped*
*4 tbsps butter*
*3 tbsps flour*
*Salt*
*Pepper*

### METHOD

Poach fish in 1¼ cups water, with lemon juice, peppercorns, bay leaf, slice of onion and parsley stalks, for 10 minutes or until just cooked. Remove from poaching liquid. Strain, reserving liquid, and cool. Melt butter in pan. Add onion and fry gently until softened. Stir in flour and cook for 1 minute. Draw off heat and gradually stir in reserved liquid, stirring continuously. Add salt and pepper to taste. Return to heat and cook for 3 minutes. Set aside to cool. Sift salt and flour into a bowl. Cut cold fat into small pieces and drop into flour. Cut fat into flour. When well cut in, use fingers to rub in completely. Mix to a firm but pliable dough with cold water. Knead on a lightly floured board until smooth. Chill for 15 minutes in the refrigerator. Roll out on a lightly floured board and line a 9-inch flan ring. Flake fish and place in bottom of prepared dough shell. Stir cream into lightly beaten egg. Add mixture to sauce gradually, and pour over fish. Arrange anchovies in a lattice over top, with a piece of olive in the center of each diamond. Bake in the oven for 20-25 minutes until golden brown. Serve hot or cold.

## FISH, ZUCCHINI AND LEMON KEBABS

Kebabs always make a nice change, and children in particular enjoy them.

Preparation Time: 30 minutes, plus chilling time
Cooking Time: about 8 minutes
Serves: 4

### INGREDIENTS

*16 small, thin sole fillets, or 8 large ones, cut in half lengthwise*
*4 tbsps olive oil*
*1 clove garlic, peeled and minced*
*Juice of ½ lemon*
*Finely grated rind of ½ lemon*
*Salt and freshly ground black pepper to taste*
*3 drops Tabasco*
*3 medium size zucchini, cut into ¼ inch slices*
*1 medium green pepper, halved, seeded and cut into 1-inch pieces*

GARNISH

*2 tbsps coarsely chopped parsley*

### METHOD

Roll up each sole fillet, jelly roll fashion, and secure with wooden picks. Place them in a shallow dish. Mix the olive oil with the garlic, lemon juice, lemon rind, salt and pepper to taste and the Tabasco. Spoon evenly over the fish. Cover and chill for 2 hours. Remove the wooden picks and carefully thread the rolled fish fillets onto kebab skewers together with the zucchini slices and pieces of green pepper, alternating them for color. Brush each threaded kebab with the lemon and oil marinade. Broil for about 8 minutes under a moderately hot broiler, carefully turning the kebabs once during cooking. Brush the kebabs during cooking with any remaining marinade. Place the kebabs on a serving dish and sprinkle with chopped parsley.

Below: Porto Sannazaro, Naples. Overleaf: a sleepy Tuscan farm.

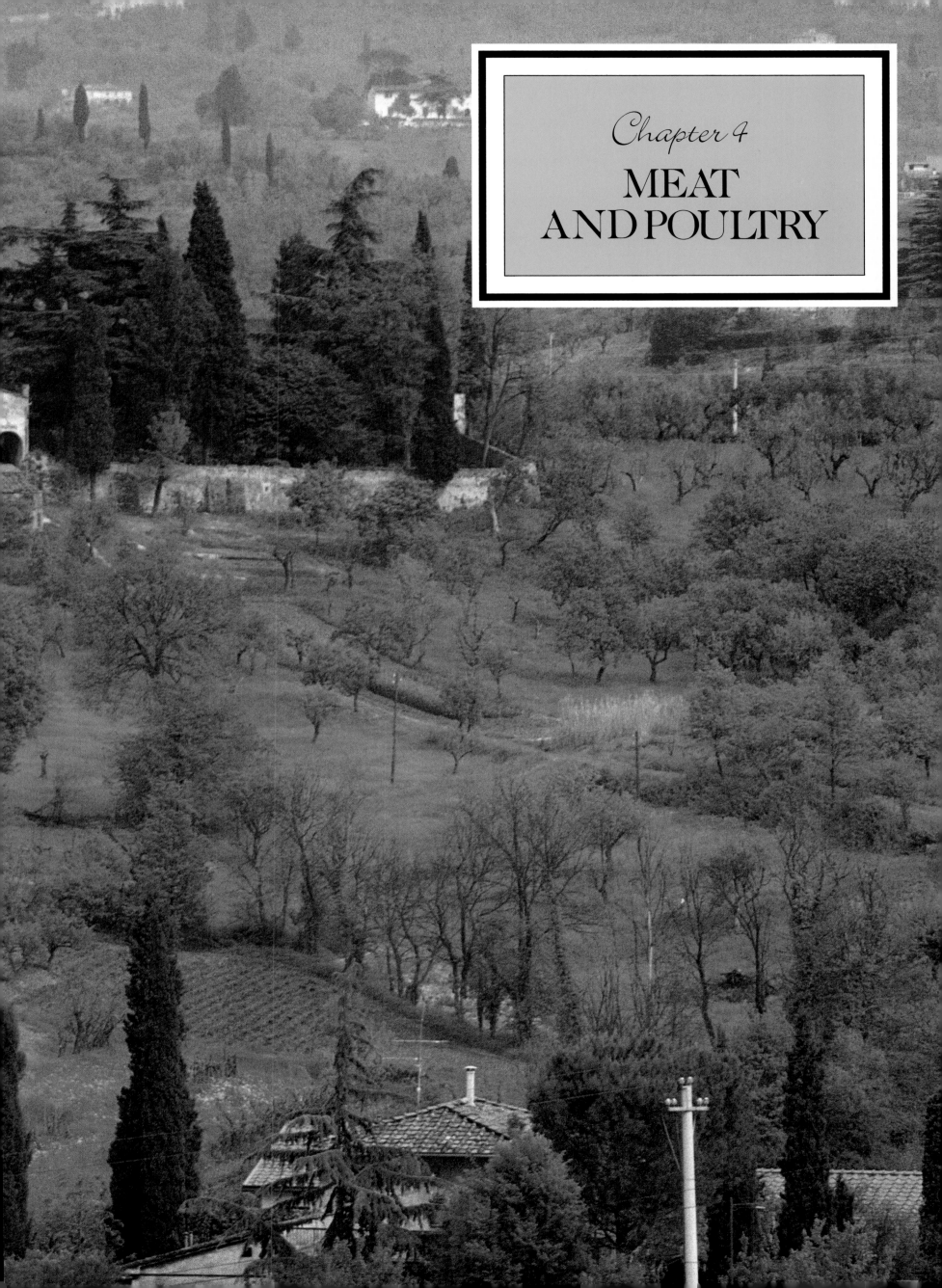

*Chapter 4*

# MEAT
# AND POULTRY

## SKEWERED VEAL BIRDS

Veal is a regular dish on Italian tables. In this unusual recipe it is served with polenta, an accompaniment almost as popular as pasta.

Preparation Time: 25 minutes
Cooking Time: 45 minutes
Serves: 4

### INGREDIENTS

*8oz lean veal steak, cubed*
*8oz fresh ham steak, cubed*
*4oz pork liver, cubed*
*4oz bacon, cubed*
*Fresh bay leaves*
*3 tbsps oil*
*7 tbsps dry white wine*
*½ cup chicken broth*

POLENTA

*2 cups water*
*2 tbsps salt*
*2 cups cornmeal*
*½ cup grated Parmesan cheese*
*Pepper*

### METHOD

Put veal, ham, liver and bacon cubes on long skewers, alternating the various kinds of meat and occasionally putting a bay leaf between one piece and another. Heat oil in a frying pan, add skewers and cook over high heat, turning occasionally. Add white wine and broth and cook for another 10 minutes, turning occasionally.

To prepare the polenta, bring the water and the salt to the boil in a large pan and gradually stir in the cornmeal. Stir well to remove any lumps. Reduce the heat to low and partially cover. Continue cooking until the polenta is thick, about 30 minutes. Stir frequently and add more water if necessary to prevent sticking. Add the cheese and adjust the seasoning. Spread into a serving dish and lay the veal skewers on top.

The Castle of Venere in the Trapani district of Sicily.

## CHICKEN CACCIATORE

The name means Chicken the Hunter's Way, that is with mushrooms. Try serving it with pasta or rice as a winter warmer.

Preparation Time: 25-30 minutes
Cooking Time: 1 hour 15 minutes
Oven Temperature: 350°F
Serves: 4-6

### INGREDIENTS

*3 tbsps oil*
*4oz mushrooms, quartered, if large*
*3lb chicken, skinned if desired and cut into pieces*
*1 onion*
*2 cloves garlic*
*½ cup vermouth*
*1 tbsp white wine vinegar*
*½ cup chicken stock*
*1 tsp oregano*
*1 sprig fresh rosemary*
*1lb canned tomatoes*
*2oz black olives, pitted*
*2 tbsps chopped parsley*
*Salt and pepper*

### METHOD

Heat the oil in a heavy-based frying pan and cook the mushrooms for about 1-2 minutes. Remove them and set aside. Brown the chicken in the oil and transfer the browned pieces to an ovenproof casserole. Chop the onion and garlic finely. Pour off all but 1 tbsp of the oil in the frying pan and reheat the pan. Cook the onion and garlic until softened but not colored. Add the vermouth and vinegar, and boil to reduce by half. Add the chicken stock, tomatoes, oregano, rosemary, salt and pepper. Break up the tomatoes and bring the sauce to the boil. Allow to cook for 2 minutes. Pour the sauce over the chicken in the casserole, cover and cook for about 1 hour. To remove the stones from the olives, roll them on a flat surface to loosen the stones and then use a swivel vegetable peeler to extract them. Alternatively, use a cherry pitter. Add mushrooms and olives during the last 5 minutes of cooking. Remove the rosemary before serving, and sprinkle with chopped parsley.

A narrow mountain road winds through the Passo di Pordoi in the Dolomites.

## SADDLE OF PORK TUSCAN STYLE

Italian dishes do not always have a large number of ingredients. Pork is instantly enlivened by the simple addition of rosemary.

Preparation Time: 10 minutes
Cooking Time: 1½-1¾ hours
Serves: 4-6

### INGREDIENTS

2½lbs pork joint
2 cloves garlic, cut into slivers
2 sprigs fresh rosemary
Salt, peppercorns
4 tbsps olive oil

### METHOD

Cut small slits in the pork and stuff with slivers of garlic and tufts of rosemary. Season with salt and freshly ground pepper. Heat 2 tbsps of the oil in a roasting pan. Add pork, pour a thin stream of remaining oil over it and roast in preheated oven 425°F for about 20 minutes. When pork is nicely browned, lower heat to 350°F and roast for another 1¼ hours, turning meat occasionally. Remove from oven, carve, arrange slices on a serving platter and serve. This dish is good either hot or cold.

## LIVER AND BACON KEBABS

Liver and bacon kebabs make an excellent meal when served with cooked vegetables in winter, or a salad in summer.

Preparation Time: 20 minutes
Cooking Time: 5-10 minutes

### INGREDIENTS

12oz piece of lamb's liver
6oz piece of bacon
½ cup mushrooms
¼ cup melted butter
¼ cup fine breadcrumbs
½ tsp paprika
Salt

### METHOD

Wipe and trim the liver. Cut it into 1-inch cubes. De-rind the bacon, cut it into thick strips, then into squares. Wipe and trim mushrooms. Preheat the broiler. Line the broiling pan with foil. Thread the bacon, liver and mushrooms onto four skewers. Brush with melted butter. Mix the breadcrumbs, paprika and salt together on a plate. Turn the kebabs in the breadcrumbs till evenly coated. Arrange on the broiler pan and broil for about 5 minutes, turning the kebabs frequently and brushing them with the fat that runs from the bacon.

## *LIVER VENEZIANA*

This recipe originated in Venice, where it was prized for being healthful as well as mouthwatering

Preparation Time: 30 minutes
Cooking Time: 4 minutes
Serves: 4-6

### INGREDIENTS

#### RISOTTO

*9oz Italian rice*
*3 tbsps butter or margarine*
*1 large onion, chopped*
*4 tbsps dry white wine*
*2 cups chicken stock*
*¼ tsp saffron*
*2 tbsps grated fresh Parmesan cheese*
*Salt and pepper*

#### LIVER

*1lb calves' or lambs' liver*
*Flour for dredging*
*3 onions, thinly sliced*
*2 tbsps butter or margarine*
*3 tbsps oil*
*Salt and pepper*
*Juice of ½ a lemon*
*1 tbsp chopped parsley*

### METHOD

Melt the butter for the risotto in a large sauté pan, add the onion and cook over gentle heat until soft but not colored. Add the rice and cook for about a minute, until the rice looks clear. Add the wine, stock, saffron and seasoning. Stir well and bring to the boil. Lower the heat and cook gently, stirring frequently until the liquid has evaporated. This will take about 20 minutes. Meanwhile, skin the liver and cut out any large tubes. Cut the liver into strips and toss in a sieve with the flour to coat. Heat the butter or margarine and 1 tbsp oil in a large sauté pan or frying pan. Cook the onions until golden. Remove the onions to a plate. Add more oil if necessary, raise the heat under the pan and add the liver. Cook, stirring constantly, for about 2 minutes. Return the onions and add the lemon juice and parsley. Cook a further 2 minutes, or until the liver is done. Season with salt and pepper and serve with the risotto. To finish the risotto, add the cheese and salt and pepper to taste when the liquid has evaporated, and toss to melt the cheese.

The Grand Canal – the busiest waterway in Venice.

## CHICKEN AND HAM CRÊPES

The combination of chicken and Fontina cheese turns an ordinary crêpe into a crespelle. Serve one as an appetizer, or a more substantial amount as a main meal.

Preparation Time: 5 minutes
Cooking Time: 30 minutes
Oven Temperature: 400°F
Serves: 4-6

### INGREDIENTS

#### CRESPELLE BATTER

*1 cup flour*
*Pinch of salt*
*2 medium eggs*
*1 cup milk*
*1 tbsp olive oil or vegetable oil*
*Oil to grease pan*

#### FILLING

*2 chicken breasts, cooked and shredded*
*2 slices cooked prosciutto, shredded*
*2 tbsps grated Fontina cheese*
*4 tbsps butter or margarine*
*3 tbsps flour*

*1 cup milk*
*Salt*
*Pepper*

#### GARNISH

*Parsley*

### METHOD

Sift flour and salt into a bowl. Make a well in the center and drop in eggs. Start to mix in eggs gradually, taking in flour from around edges. When becoming stiff, add a little milk until all flour has been incorporated. Beat to a smooth batter, then add remaining milk. Stir in oil. Cover bowl, and leave in a cool place for 30 minutes. Heat small frying pan, or 7-inch crêpe pan. Wipe over with oil. When hot, add enough batter mixture to cover base of pan when rolled. Pour off any excess batter. When brown on underside, loosen and turn over with a spatula, and brown on other side. Pile on a plate and cover with a clean towel until needed. Melt butter in pan. Stir in flour and cook for 1 minute. Remove from heat and gradually stir in milk. Return to heat, bring to the boil, and cook for 3 minutes, stirring continuously. Add cheese, chicken, ham and salt and pepper and stir until heated through. Do not re-boil. Divide the mixture evenly between the pancakes and roll up or fold into triangles. Place in a baking dish and cover with aluminum foil. Heat in a hot oven for 10 minutes. Garnish with parsley. Serve immediately.

Facing page: fountains in the gardens of the Villa d'Este, Tivoli.

## PORK ROULADES WITH POLENTA

Polenta gives this dish its particular Italian feel and the roulades make it attractive enough for any occasion.

Preparation Time: 20 minutes
Cooking Time: 1 hour for the polenta, 20 minutes for the roulades
Serves: 4-8

### INGREDIENTS

*8oz coarse yellow cornmeal*
*6 cups chicken stock*
*Salt and white pepper*

ROULADES

*8 pork escalopes or steaks*
*8 slices Parma ham*
*4 large cup mushrooms*
*4 tbsps grated Parmesan cheese*
*1 tbsp chopped fresh sage*
*Seasoned flour for dredging*
*4 tbsps olive oil*
*1 small onion, finely chopped*
*2 sticks celery, finely chopped*
*1 clove garlic, minced*
*6 tbsps brown stock*
*½ cup dry white wine*
*4oz canned plum tomatoes, drained and juice reserved*
*1 tsp tomato paste*
*Salt and pepper*
*6 tbsps dry Marsala*
*Fresh sage leaves for garnish*

### METHOD

Bring the chicken stock for the polenta to the boil in a large stock pot and start adding the cornmeal in a very slow, steady stream, stirring continuously. Add salt and pepper and continue cooking over very low heat, stirring frequently, for about 55 minutes.

Flatten the pork escalopes or steaks and place a slice of Parma ham on top of each. Chop the mushrooms and divide among the pork escalopes, spooning on top of the ham slices. Sprinkle over the Parmesan cheese and the fresh sage.

Fold the sides of the pork escalopes into the center to seal them, and roll up the pork jelly roll fashion. Secure each roll with a wooden pick. Dredge each roulade in flour, shaking off the excess.

Heat the olive oil in a large sauté pan or frying pan and add the pork roulades, seam side down first. Cook on all sides until nicely browned. Remove the roulades and keep them warm

Add the onion and celery to the oil in the pan and cook until lightly browned. Add the garlic and all the remaining ingredients except the Marsala. Reserve the juice from the tomatoes for later use if necessary. Bring the sauce to the boil, breaking up the tomatoes. Return the roulades to the pan, cover and cook over moderate heat for about 15-20 minutes or until the pork is completely cooked. Add reserved tomato juice, as necessary, if liquid is drying out.

When the pork is cooked, remove to a dish and keep it warm. Add the Marsala to the sauce and bring to the boil. Allow to boil for 5-10 minutes. The sauce may be puréed in a food processor and also sieved if desired.

To assemble the dish, spoon the polenta on a serving plate. Remove the wooden picks from the roulades and place on top of the polenta. Spoon the sauce over the meat and garnish the dish with fresh sage leaves.

The peace and tranquility of Lake Garda attract many visitors to its shores.

## DUCK CASSEROLE

Duck is excellent cooked in this manner as it remains tender and succulent

Preparation Time: 10 minutes
Cooking Time: 1 hour
Serves: 4-6

### INGREDIENTS

*1 duckling weighing about 5lb*
*1 medium onion*
*2 cloves*
*1 bay leaf*
*2 sage leaves*
*½ cup olive oil*
*¼ cup wine vinegar*
*¼ cup dry white wine*
*Parsley for garnish*
*Salt and pepper*

### METHOD

Joint the duckling. In a deep saucepan, place the chopped duck liver, heart and gizzard, the onion stuck with cloves, bay leaf and sage. Place the duck on top and pour over the olive oil, wine vinegar and white wine. Season with salt and pepper. Cover and simmer for about 1 hour, or until the duck is tender. Put the joints on a serving dish and keep warm. Remove the cloves and the bay leaf, and blend the remaining ingredients in the casserole with the cooking liquid. Return to the heat, pour over the duck and garnish with chopped parsley.

Facing page: the harbor of Vietri sul Mare on the Gulf of Salerno.

## *VEAL WITH CUCUMBER*

Veal is a great favorite in Italy and a lot of imagination is employed in putting it to best use.

Preparation Time: 20-25 minutes
Serves: 4

### INGREDIENTS

*8-12oz fillet veal, cubed*
*Salt and pepper*
*1 tbsp cornstarch*
*¼ cup water*
*½ cup mushrooms*
*2 eating apples, peeled cored and sliced*
*1 cucumber, peeled and diced*
*1 green pepper, cored, seeded and sliced*
*1 red pepper, cored, seeded and sliced*
*½ cup cooked rice*

Facing page: the Arco
di Pace in Milan.

SWEET AND SOUR SAUCE

*1 tbsp cornstarch*
*2 tbsps sugar*
*2 tsps soy sauce*
*3 tbsps vinegar*
*⅔ cup chicken stock*

### METHOD

Toss the veal in seasoned cornstarch and fry in the butter until golden. Remove and keep warm. Fry the mushrooms, apple slices and cucumber. Fry the peppers. Return the meat to the pan. Cover and cook for 10 minutes until the meat is tender. Stir in the cooked rice. Transfer to a serving dish and keep hot. Mix the sweet and sour sauce ingredients together, add to the pan and, stirring gently, boil for 2-3 minutes, until the sauce is transparent. Pour the sauce over the veal and cucumber mixture. This can be served as a meal in its own right, or served with a vegetable dish if required.

## SICILIAN ROAST LAMB

"Agnello al Forno" makes a wonderful centerpiece for the family's Sunday roast. Serve it with a variety of vegetables and a good bottle of red wine for the perfect meal.

Preparation Time: 5 minutes
Cooking Time: 1½ hours
Oven Temperature: 375°F
Serves: 4-6

### INGREDIENTS

*1 leg of lamb, about 3½lbs in weight*
*¼ cup boiled ham, diced*
*1-2 sprigs rosemary*
*1 stick butter*
*3 tbsps soft breadcrumbs*
*½lb grated cheese*
*Salt and pepper*

### METHOD

With a sharp knife, make incisions into the surface of the lamb, about 1 inch deep. Into each cut push a piece of ham and two or three leaves of rosemary. Put the meat into a large baking pan, season with salt and pepper and pour the melted butter over the meat. Mix the breadcrumbs and the grated cheese and spread evenly over the meat, pressing down well. Roast in preheated oven, basting from time to time, for about 1½ hours. (If you have any cooked meat left over, it is delicious used in lasagne.)

## PIQUANT STEAK

Unlike Americans, Italians enjoy their steak mixed with a sauce. Here, tomatoes and anchovies provide the Italian flavor.

Preparation Time: 15 minutes
Cooking Time: 15-20 minutes
Serves: 4

### INGREDIENTS

*3 anchovy fillets, chopped*
*¾ cup chopped tomato pulp, skin and seeds removed,*
*or fresh tomato*
*1½lbs steak (sirloin or butt)*
*3 tbsps olive oil*
*2 tbsps capers*
*½ cup dry white wine*
*Salt and pepper*

### METHOD

Cut the steak into strips about 3 inches long and ½ inch thick. Mix anchovy fillets and tomato pulp. Brown steak quickly in oil and remove to a platter. Add tomato pulp mixture and capers to pan juices. Heat until bubbly. Stir in wine and pinch of pepper and simmer until sauce is thick. Season to taste with salt. Return steak to pan and cook to desired degree, turning several times in sauce and making sure that it is not overcooked. Salt lightly and serve immediately with pan juices spooned over. Serve with freshly cooked pasta.

## *FIN AND FEATHER*

Chicken is always popular; combining it with salmon makes it absolutely irresistible.

Preparation Time: 20 minutes
Cooking Time: 15-20 minutes
Oven Temperature: 350°F
Serves: 4

### INGREDIENTS

*4 chicken supremes (boned chicken breasts)*
*3oz fresh salmon, or canned red salmon*
*White wine*
*4 anchovies*
*⅔ cup olive oil*
*2 egg yolks*
*Salt and pepper*
*1½ tbsps lemon juice*
*1 tbsp chopped parsley*

GARNISH

*4 small dill pickles*
*1 tbsp capers*
*Curly endive*

### METHOD

Buy prepared chicken breasts. Put them on a sheet of aluminum foil and sprinkle over salt, pepper and a little white wine. Seal foil well. Put into a baking dish and bake in the oven for about 15 minutes, or until cooked through. Open foil packet and allow to cool. Reserve juices from the chicken. Poach the fresh salmon (or drain canned salmon) and remove bones. Put the salmon and anchovies into a food processor bowl or blender and work until broken up. Work in the egg yolks, and salt and pepper. With the machine running, add the oil gradually. Add lemon juice to taste and adjust seasoning. Stir in the cooking liquid from the chicken to give the sauce the consistency of thin cream – if it is too thick, add a few drops of milk or water. Put cold chicken breasts onto a plate and coat with the sauce. Before serving, garnish the dish with capers and pickles. Serve with a green salad or a cold rice salad.

## LIVER WITH ORANGES

Liver plays an important part in a healthful diet; when complemented with oranges, its nutritional value is even greater.

Preparation Time: 20 minutes
Cooking Time: 15-20 minutes
Serves: 4

### INGREDIENTS

*12oz liver, sliced*
*2 tbsps flour*
*Salt and pepper*
*2 tbsps butter*
*1 tbsp olive oil*
*1 onion, sliced*
*1 small clove garlic*
*½ cup brown stock*
*Juice and grated rind of 1 orange*
*2 oranges, peeled and sliced, for garnish*

### METHOD

Dredge the liver slices with flour and season with salt and pepper. Heat the oil in a sauté pan and drop in the butter. When the fat is hot, add the liver and cook until browned on both sides, about 5 minutes. Cook in two batches if necessary. Remove the liver and add the onions to the pan. Cook until beginning to brown and add the garlic, minced. Add any remaining flour and pour on the stock and orange juice. Add the orange rind and stir to mix well, scraping any sediment off the bottom of the pan. Add the liver, cover the pan, and simmer for 10-15 minutes, or until the liver is tender. Serve with rice and pasta, and garnish with orange slices.

Facing page: tourists explore a quiet canal in Venice – by gondola, of course!

## VEAL CASSEROLE

Veal is the most commonly used meat in Italian cooking, and although it is expensive, its taste and texture make it well worth the extra expense.

Preparation Time: 30 minutes
Cooking Time: 50 minutes
Serves: 4

### INGREDIENTS

*1½lbs veal shoulder, cubed*
*Salt and pepper*
*1 cup chicken stock*
*1 sprig marjoram*
*1 bay leaf*
*2 large carrots*
*2 sticks celery, chopped*
*3 tbsps butter or margarine*
*3 tbsps flour*
*1 tbsp chopped parsley*
*½ tbsp chopped marjoram*
*½ cup stuffed green olives*
*4 slices of bread*
*4 tbsps oil*

### METHOD

Season the veal. Bring the chicken stock to the boil, add the meat, sprig of marjoram, bay leaf, carrots and celery, cover and allow to simmer for 45 minutes. Melt the butter in a small pan and stir in the flour. Cook until golden brown and pour in the stock from the veal. Cook until thickened and pour over the veal. Add the parsley and marjoram and adjust the seasoning. Stir in the olives and keep warm. Heat the oil in a frying pan. Cut the bread into triangles and fry until golden brown on both sides. Drain well and serve with the veal.

# PIQUANT PORK CHOPS WITH FENNEL

The humble pork chop is greatly enhanced by the flavor of fennel.

Preparation Time: 30 minutes
Cooking Time: 1 hour 10 minutes
Oven Temperature: 350°F
Serves: 4

## INGREDIENTS

*4 pork chops*
*1 tbsp oil*
*1 small onion, peeled and chopped*
*1 tbsp brown sugar*
*1 tbsp fennel seed*
*1 tbsp tomato paste*
*1 cup stock*
*1 cup red wine*
*2 tbsps lemon juice*

## METHOD

Put the chops in a baking pan, or a wide, shallow casserole dish and bake, uncovered, at 350°F for about 20 minutes. Meanwhile, heat the oil, add the onion and fry until browned. Add the sugar, fennel seed and tomato paste. Mix well then add the stock and stir till boiling. Add the wine and lemon juice and check seasoning. Pour off any excess fat from the chops and pour the sauce over them. Cover, and continue cooking in the oven at 350°F for about 40-45 minutes.

Facing page: the Temple of Fortuna Augusta, Pompeii.

# CHICKEN WITH PEPPERS

"Pollo con Peperoni" is a common mid-week meal in Italy. Tasty and filling, it cannot help but please a hungry family.

Preparation Time: 15 minutes
Cooking Time: 1 hour
Serves: 4

## INGREDIENTS

*1 chicken (weighing about 2½lbs)*
*4 to 5 fleshy green and red peppers*
*1 large onion, sliced*
*2 tbsps butter*
*3 tbsps olive oil*
*Salt, pepper*
*½ cup dry white wine*
*4 cups fresh chopped tomato pulp, skins and seeds removed*
*1 cup chicken broth*
*¼ cup chopped fresh basil*

## METHOD

Cut chicken into serving pieces. Roast peppers over heat until skin blisters. Rub skin off with a kitchen towel. Remove seeds and cut peppers into 1-inch wide strips. Sauté onion in butter and oil until soft. Add chicken pieces and and cook until brown, turning often. Season with salt and pepper and, when chicken has browned, add wine. Simmer until wine has evaporated, then add peppers, tomatoes and another pinch of salt and pepper. Add broth. Cover and simmer over low heat, stirring occasionally, for about 45 minutes, or until chicken is tender. Remove from heat and sprinkle with chopped basil (or parsley if you prefer). Pan juices may be skimmed of fat and boiled until reduced to half their original volume. Pour pan juices over chicken.

Facing page: the 14,691-foot-high Monte Cervino, probably better known as the Matterhorn.

# TAGLIATELLE WITH CREAMY LIVER SAUCE

Tagliatelle is one of the most favored pastas; it is fun to eat and very healthful when combined with a liver sauce.

Preparation Time: 10 minutes
Cooking Time: 15 minutes

## INGREDIENTS

*1 9oz package tagliatelle*
*4 tbsps olive oil*
*2 medium onions, peeled and sliced*
*1 clove garlic, minced*
*¾ cup mushrooms, sliced*
*1lb chicken livers, cleaned and sliced*
*⅓ cup cream*
*2 eggs, beaten*
*1 tbsp chopped parsley*
*Salt and pepper*

## METHOD

In a large frying pan, cook onions and garlic gently in oil until softened. Add mushrooms and cook for 3 minutes. Add chicken livers to onions and mushrooms, and cook until lightly browned. Remove from heat and stir in cream. Return to low heat, and cook, uncovered, for further 2 minutes. Remove from heat, and stir in lightly beaten eggs. Season with salt and pepper to taste. Meanwhile, cook the tagliatelle in plenty of boiling salted water for 10 minutes, or until tender but still firm, stirring occasionally. Drain tagliatelle, toss in oil and black pepper. Serve sauce over tagliatelle and sprinkle with parsley.

Facing page: a crowded waterfront at Mondello, near Palermo, in Sicily.

## BEEF SCALLOPS TUSCAN STYLE

Beef is enhanced by Marsala, a dessert wine from Sicily. If you cannot obtain any, substitute sherry.

Preparation Time: 15 minutes
Cooking Time: 15 minutes
Serves: 4-6

### INGREDIENTS

*1½lbs boneless beef round, sliced ¼ inch thick*
*Salt*
*All-purpose flour*
*1 egg, beaten*
*1½ tbsps butter*
*2 tbsps olive oil*
*⅓ cup Marsala*
*1 tbsp tomato paste*
*4 anchovy fillets, chopped*
*1 tbsp capers, chopped*
*4 tomatoes, quartered*

### METHOD

Pound the beef until very thin, and sprinkle with salt and flour on both sides. Dip in beaten egg. Heat butter and oil in a large frying pan. Brown beef slices on both sides. Add Marsala, raise heat slightly, and simmer until wine evaporates. Place beef slices on a platter and keep warm. Into same pan, add tomato paste mixed with ½ cup water and simmer for 5 minutes. Add anchovies and capers and simmer for 2 minutes more. Put beef back in the pan with the sauce and simmer for 2-3 minutes over a low heat. Garnish with tomatoes.

## VEAL WITH MOZZARELLA

Although simple to make, this dish is tasty enough to serve on almost any occasion.

Preparation Time: 5 minutes
Cooking Time: 15-20 minutes
Serves: 6

### INGREDIENTS

*6 slices boneless veal (or 12 small scalloppine)*
*2 tbsps butter*
*2 tbsps olive oil*
*Salt and pepper*
*Juice of ½ lemon*
*6 slices of prosciutto crudo*
*6 slices Mozzarella or Scamorza*

### METHOD

Pound veal slices, trim them so they are about the same size and shape, then brown in butter and oil. Sprinkle with salt and pepper. Let meat cook to a golden brown, then sprinkle with lemon juice. A few minutes before serving, place a slice of prosciutto and one of Mozzarella or Scamorza on each veal slice. Heat until cheese melts and serve immediately.

## CRESPELLE WITH CHICKEN AND TONGUE

Crespelles are Italian pancakes. The chicken and tongue in this recipe make them filling enough to serve as a main meal.

Preparation Time: 40 minutes
Cooking Time: 20 minutes
Oven Temperature: 450°F
Serves: 4

### INGREDIENTS

#### 12 CRESPELLE

*3 eggs*
*¾ cup flour*
*Pinch of salt*
*1 cup water*
*½ tsp olive oil*
*2 tbsps butter or margarine, melted*

#### FILLING

*8oz chicken, cooked and shredded*
*8oz tongue, cut into strips*

#### BECHAMEL SAUCE

*2 tbsps butter or margarine*
*1 tbsp flour*
*1 cup milk*

**To infuse:**
*4 peppercorns*
*1 bay leaf*
*Slice of onion*
*Salt*
*Pepper*

### METHOD

#### To make crespelle

Sift flour with a pinch of salt. Break eggs into a bowl, and whisk. Add flour gradually, whisking all the time until the mixture is smooth. Add water and stir in well. Add oil, and mix. Cover bowl with a damp cloth, and leave in a cool place for 30 minutes. Heat a crêpe pan, or 7-inch frying pan. Grease lightly with melted butter, and put a good tablespoon of batter in the center. Roll the pan to coat the surface evenly. Fry until crespelle is brown on the underside. Loosen edge with a spatula, turn over and brown the other side. Stack and wrap in a clean cloth until needed.

#### To make bechamel sauce

Warm milk with peppercorns, bay leaf and slice of onion. Remove from heat, and let stand for 5 minutes. Strain. Heat butter in pan. Stir in flour and cook for 1 minute. Remove from heat, and gradually stir in two-thirds of the milk. Return to heat, and stir continuously until boiling. Simmer for 3 minutes. Add salt and pepper to taste. Put half of the sauce in a bowl, and add the chicken and tongue. Mix together. Beat remaining milk into remaining sauce.

Lay one crespelle on a plate, and top with a layer of chicken and tongue. Cover with another crespelle, and continue, finishing with a crespelle. Pour over sauce, and bake in preheated oven for 10 minutes. Serve immediately.

Facing page: bright summer colors at the popular resort of Rapallo, in Liguria. Overleaf: autumn near Misurina in the Dolomite Mountains.

Chapter 5

# VEGETABLES AND SALADS

## APPLE AND NUT SALAD

Simple salads are often the best, and this one is certainly a good example.

Preparation Time: 10 minutes
Serves: 4

### INGREDIENTS

*Salt and pepper*
*Pinch of dry mustard*
*3 tbsps corn or olive oil*
*1 tbsp wine vinegar*
*3 red eating apples, peeled and cored*
*8 sticks of celery, scrubbed and chopped*
*¼ cup chopped nuts*
*Chopped fresh parsley to garnish*

### METHOD

Put salt, pepper, mustard, oil and vinegar into a screw-topped jar and shake well. Put the apples and celery in a bowl with the chopped nuts. Pour the dressing over the apples and celery and toss well. Spoon into a serving dish and garnish with chopped parsley.

## SALAD OF PASTA QUILLS

Salads play an important part in Italian cuisine. This classic recipe is a mixture of some of Italy's favorite ingredients.

Preparation Time: 15 minutes
Cooking Time: 15 minutes
Serves: 4

### INGREDIENTS

*1½ cups penne*
*3 tomatoes, quartered*
*¼lb green beans, cooked*
*½ cucumber, cut into batons*
*1 7oz can tuna fish, drained and flaked*
*12 black olives, halved, with stones removed*
*6-8 anchovy fillets, drained, and soaked in milk if desired*
*½ cup bottled oil and vinegar dressing*

### METHOD

Cook penne in plenty of boiling salted water until tender but still firm. Rinse in cold water; drain, and leave to dry. Put flaked tuna in the base of a salad dish. Toss pasta together with tomatoes, cucumber, green beans, olives, and anchovies, and then pour over oil and vinegar dressing. Mix together well.

Facing page: sunset gilds the waters that flow in front of the church of Santa Maria della Salute and the Customs House. Overleaf: the town of Livigno, near the border with Switzerland, shows the Swiss influence in its chalet-style buildings.

## BAKED ASPARAGUS ITALIAN STYLE

Asparagus is always a treat; prepared the Italian way it is even more mouthwatering.

Preparation Time: 10 minutes
Cooking Time: 20 minutes
Oven Temperature: 400°F
Serves: 4

### INGREDIENTS

*24 asparagus*
*4 thick slices prosciutto, crudo, fat and lean, or ham*
*6 tbsps butter*
*¾ cup grated Parmesan*
*4 slices toast (made by frying bread in butter)*
*Salt*

### METHOD

Clean asparagus and trim tough ends. Remove scales. Tie asparagus in a bundle. Cook asparagus standing upright with tips above boiling water. Use your coffee pot for this. Drain while still "al dente", untie the bundle and let asparagus cool completely. Wrap 6 asparagus tips in each slice of ham and arrange the rolls in a lightly buttered shallow baking dish. Pour about 2 tbsps of melted butter over them, sprinkle with grated Parmesan, then pour 1 tbsp more melted butter over the Parmesan. Put the dish in the preheated oven and bake until surface is well browned, about 15 minutes. Meanwhile, brown the bread slices in remaining butter and transfer them to a serving dish. Put ham asparagus rolls on each slice of toast and serve.

## TUNA AND TOMATO SALAD

This quick salad is the perfect solution to the problem of serving unexpected lunch guests.

Preparation Time: 10 minutes
Cooking Time: 15 minutes
Serves: 4

### INGREDIENTS

3 cups pasta shells
1 7oz can tuna fish, flaked
6 tomatoes
1 tbsp fresh chopped basil or marjoram, or 1 tsp dried basil or oregano
6 tbsps vinaigrette dressing

### METHOD

Mix herbs with vinaigrette dressing. Cook pasta shells in a large saucepan of boiling salted water until tender – about 10 minutes. Rinse with cold water, and drain, shaking off excess water. Toss with 3 tablespoons of vinaigrette dressing. Leave to cool. Meanwhile, slice enough of the tomatoes to arrange around the outside of the serving-dish. Chop the rest, and pour the remaining vinaigrette dressing over them, and place in the center of the dish. Add tuna to the pasta shells, and toss gently. Serve in the center of the dish over the chopped tomatoes.

## PEPPER SALAD WITH CAPERS

Capers are a popular ingredient in Italian cooking. Here they provide a lively contrast to the flavor of the peppers.

Preparation Time: 30 minutes, plus 1 hour refrigeration
Serves: 4-6

### INGREDIENTS

3 large peppers, red, green and yellow
6 tbsps olive oil
1 clove garlic, peeled and finely chopped
Basil leaves, roughly chopped
Fresh marjoram roughly chopped
2 tbsps capers
1 tbsp white wine vinegar

### METHOD

Cut the peppers in half and remove the core and seeds. Press with the palm of the hand or the back of a knife to flatten. Brush the skin side with oil and place the peppers under a preheated broiler. Broil the peppers until the skins are well charred. Wrap in a towel and leave for 15 minutes. Unwrap and peel off the charred skin. Cut the peppers into thick strips and arrange on a serving dish. Scatter over the chopped garlic, basil leaves, marjoram and capers. Mix together the remaining olive oil with the vinegar and salt and pepper and pour over the salad. Refrigerate for 1 hour before serving.

## EGG AND MELON SALAD

This attractive salad is sure to become a summer favorite.

Preparation Time: 30-40 minutes
Serves: 4

### INGREDIENTS

*1 small cabbage*
*1 firm, ripe melon*
*1 orange*
*Salt and pepper*
*2 carrots, peeled and grated*
*4 hard-cooked eggs*
*Few sprigs of watercress*
*Few leaves of Belgian endive*
*8 radishes*

#### COOKED SALAD DRESSING

*1 tsp flour*
*1 tbsp sugar*
*Salt and pepper*
*½ tsp mustard powder*
*1 large egg, beaten*
*2 tbsps water*
*2 tbsps vinegar*
*1 tsp butter*

### METHOD

To prepare the dressing, combine the flour, sugar, mustard and seasoning in a heavy-based saucepan. Mix in the egg to form a smooth paste. Add the water, vinegar and butter and stir over a low heat until the sauce begins to thicken. Remove from the heat, stir thoroughly and, if necessary, strain to remove any lumps. Cool in the refrigerator. Chop the cabbage very finely. Cube the melon. Peel the orange and cut the segments into pieces. Combine these ingredients with the grated carrots in a mixing bowl. Season as required. Pour over the cooled dressing and spoon the salad mixture onto a large salad dish. Shell and slice the hard-cooked eggs and arrange them with the watercress and Belgian endive leaves round the salad. Cut the radishes into floral shapes and garnish the salad and serve.

Right: the Fountain of Neptune in the Piazza Navona in Rome. Overleaf: Palermo Cathedral by night.

Facing page: the quiet,
unspoilt beauty of
Atrani, on the Sorrento
peninsula.

## CREAMED SPINACH

Spinach is a suitable accompaniment to many dishes, and is especially tasty when it is creamed.

Cooking Time: 15-20 minutes
Serves: 4-6

### INGREDIENTS

*3lbs fresh spinach, washed and coarse stalks removed*
*2-4 tbsps butter*
*3 tbsps light cream*
*Salt and pepper*
*Pinch of powdered nutmeg*

### METHOD

Put the washed spinach in a saucepan with a little water. Heat gently, turning the spinach occasionally. Bring to the boil and cook gently for 10-15 minutes, until very soft.

Drain thoroughly and pass through a sieve or use a blender. Add butter, cream, seasoning and nutmeg to the purée. Return to the pan and reheat. Serve in a warmed dish.

## MUSHROOM SALAD

Raw mushrooms have a crunchy texture and pungent flavor which is deliciously different from the cooked variety.

Preparation Time: 1 hour 10 minutes
Cooking Time: 15 minutes
Serves: 4

### INGREDIENTS

*3 cups farfalle (pasta butterflies/bows)*
*1 cup mushrooms, sliced*
*5 tbsps olive oil*
*Juice of 2 lemons*
*1 tsp fresh chopped basil*
*1 tsp fresh chopped parsley*
*Salt*
*Pepper*

### METHOD

Mix oil together with lemon juice and fresh herbs. Put the sliced mushrooms into a bowl, and pour over 4 tbsps of the dressing. Leave for 1 hour. Cook the pasta in a large saucepan of boiling salted water for 10 minutes, or until tender. Rinse in cold water, and drain. Toss with the rest of the dressing, and leave to cool. Fold mushrooms and pasta together gently, adding salt and freshly-ground black pepper to taste. Sprinkle with parsley.

A spectacular view across Lake Garda.

### STUFFED TOMATOES HOME-STYLE

This quick, economical dish is surprisingly tasty, either as an appetizer or a snack.

Preparation Time: 15 minutes
Cooking Time: 20 minutes
Oven Temperature: 350°F
Serves: 4-6

### INGREDIENTS

8 medium tomatoes
Salt and pepper
1 small onion, chopped
9 tbsps butter
3 cups soft breadcrumbs
½ cup grated Parmesan
A few basil leaves, chopped
6 sprigs parsley, chopped
2 anchovy fillets
¼ cup pine nuts, ground in a mortar

### METHOD

Cut a thin slice off the tops of the tomatoes. Scoop out the seeds, then squeeze tomato cups lightly over a bowl to catch juice. Sprinkle tomato cups lightly with salt and invert them on a rack set over a pan. Reserve juice. Sauté onion in ¼ cup of the butter until golden. Combine onion and drippings, breadcrumbs, grated Parmesan, basil, parsley, anchovy fillets and pine nuts. Sprinkle with salt and pepper and stir in reserved tomato juice. Mix well. Arrange tomato cups side by side in a buttered baking dish, stuff with filling. Dot with remaining butter and bake in preheated oven for 20 minutes, or until tomatoes are tender but still hold their shape.

## GIANFOTTERE SALAD

Vegetarians in particular will enjoy this tasty salad with its mixture of healthful ingredients.

Preparation Time: 40 minutes
Cooking Time: 30 minutes
Serves: 4

### INGREDIENTS

*3 cups pasta spirals*
*1 eggplant*
*1 zucchini*
*1 sweet red pepper*
*1 green pepper*
*2 tomatoes*
*1 onion*
*4 tbsps olive oil*
*1 clove garlic*
*Salt*
*Pepper*

### METHOD

Cut eggplant into ½-inch slices. Sprinkle with salt and leave for 30 minutes. Skin the tomatoes by putting them into boiling water for 20 seconds, and then rinsing in cold water and peeling skins off. Chop roughly. Cut zucchini into ½-inch slices. Remove cores and seeds from peppers, and chop roughly. Peel and chop onion. Heat 3 tbsps olive oil in pan, and fry onion gently until transparent, but not colored. Meanwhile, rinse salt from eggplant and pat dry with absorbent paper. Chop roughly. Add eggplant, zucchini, peppers, tomatoes and garlic to onion, and fry gently for 20 minutes. Season with salt and pepper. Allow to cool.

Meanwhile, cook pasta spirals in plenty of boiling salted water for 10 minutes, or until tender but still firm. Rinse in cold water and drain well, and toss in remaining 1 tbsp olive oil. Toss vegetables together with pasta spirals.

## STUFFED ZUCCHINI

As a lively snack or appetizer, ''Zucchini Ripieni'' is sure to become a firm family favorite.

Preparation Time: 10 minutes
Cooking Time: 40-45 minutes
Oven Temperature: 350°F
Serves: 6

### INGREDIENTS

*3½lbs zucchini (12 small or 6 large)*
*½ cup diced cooked ham*
*2 tbsps chopped parsley*
*¼ cup chopped fresh basil leaves*
*2 tbsps dry breadcrumbs approx.*
*⅔ cup grated Parmesan cheese*
*2 eggs*
*Nutmeg*
*Salt, pepper*
*5 tbsps butter*
*1 tbsp flour*
*1 cup milk*

### METHOD

Cut ends off zucchini and trim them to same length. Wash and drain. Boil zucchini in lightly salted water for 10 minutes, or until half cooked. Drain. Slice in half lengthwise and remove pulp, reserving it in a bowl. Reserve shells (½-inch thick). Mix ham, parsley and basil with chopped zucchini pulp. Add breadcrumbs, all of the grated Parmesan except for 2 tbsps, eggs, freshly grated nutmeg and salt and pepper to taste. Mix these ingredients thoroughly and set aside. Melt ¼ cup of the butter and stir in the flour. Gradually stir in milk. Stir over low heat until sauce bubbles and thickens. Stir sauce into zucchini mixture. Add more breadcrumbs if mixture is not thick enough to spoon. Using a spoon, fill zucchini shells with the mixture. Arrange them side by side in a buttered shallow baking dish. Sprinkle with remaining grated Parmesan and bake in a preheated oven, 350°F, for ½ hour. Serve hot in baking dish.

Facing page: the Ponte Vecchio in Florence is lined with jewellers' shops. Overleaf: the Spanish Steps, leading to the Church of Trinita dei Monti in Rome.

Facing page: the cloister of San Francesco in Sorrento, Campania.

## CHICORY, CHICKEN AND MUSHROOM SALAD

Colorful and impressive, this salad is the perfect choice for summer entertaining.

Preparation Time: 40 minutes, plus standing time
Cooking Time: 18-20 minutes
Serves: 4

### INGREDIENTS

*4 chicken breasts, boned and skinned*
*6 tbsps olive oil*
*1 clove garlic, peeled and minced*
*Salt and freshly ground black pepper to taste*
*2 medium-size heads chicory*
*4 large cooked asparagus tips*
*4oz firm white mushrooms, thinly sliced*
*2 tbsps white wine vinegar*
*1 tbsp chopped fresh sage (optional)*

GARNISH

*Sprig fresh basil*

### METHOD

Slice the chicken breasts thinly. Heat half the olive oil in a large, shallow pan. Add the chicken slices, garlic and salt and pepper to taste and fry gently for 5 minutes; flip the chicken slices over and fry for a further 3-4 minutes. Meanwhile, prepare the salad ingredients. Cut the heads of chicory into pieces and arrange on a large, flat plate. Arrange the asparagus tips and mushroom slices between the wedges of chicory. Mix the wine vinegar with the remaining olive oil, salt and pepper to taste and the chopped sage. Spoon the dressing evenly over the salad and top with the fried chicken slices and their juices. Garnish with basil. Serve immediately.

## CHICKEN SALAD WITH PASTA SHELLS

Crispy vegetables and chicken make a perfect summer salad when something quick and appetizing is called for.

Preparation Time: 10 minutes
Cooking Time: 15 minutes
Serves: 4

### INGREDIENTS

1¼ cups soup pasta shells
8oz or 1 cup cooked chicken, shredded
1 7oz can corn, drained
1 stick celery, sliced
1 sweet red pepper, cored, seeds removed, and diced
1 green pepper, cored, seeds removed, and diced

#### DRESSING

1 tbsp mayonnaise
2 tbsps vinegar
Salt
Pepper

### METHOD

Cook pasta in plenty of boiling salted water until just tender. Drain well, and leave to cool. Meanwhile, combine mayonnaise with vinegar and salt and pepper to taste. When the pasta is cool, add chicken, corn, celery and peppers. Toss well and serve with the dressing.

## MUSHROOMS AND TOMATOES

As an accompaniment to pizza, this vegetable dish is unbeatable.

Preparation Time: 10 minutes, plus chilling time
Cooking Time: 13 minutes
Serves: 4

### INGREDIENTS

1lb tomatoes, skinned, seeded and chopped
½ cup red wine
2 tbsps tomato paste
Salt and freshly ground black pepper to taste
1 clove garlic, peeled and finely chopped
2 green onions, finely chopped
2 tbsps raisins
8oz small mushrooms

#### TO SERVE

Crusty bread or rolls

### METHOD

Put the chopped tomatoes, red wine, tomato paste, salt and pepper to taste, and the garlic into a shallow pan. Simmer for 6-8 minutes. Add the green onions, raisins and mushrooms; cover the pan and simmer for 5 minutes. Allow to cool and then chill very thoroughly. Serve in small, shallow dishes, accompanied by crusty bread.

Chapter 6

# DESSERTS

## HONEY VERMICELLI

Honey is often used as a sweetener in Italian cooking; mixed with vermicelli, the result is authentic Italian cooking at its best.

Preparation Time: 1 hour 15 minutes
Serves: 4

### INGREDIENTS

*½lb vermicelli*
*4 tbsps butter*
*3 tbsps clear honey*
*2 tsps sesame seeds*
*¼ tsp ground cinnamon*

SAUCE

*½ cup heavy cream*
*½ cup soured cream*

### METHOD

Cook vermicelli in boiling salted water for 5 minutes or until tender, stirring regularly with a fork to separate noodles. Drain, and spread out to dry on a wire rack covered with absorbent paper or a tea-towel. Leave for about an hour. Make sauce by mixing soured cream and heavy cream together. Melt butter in frying pan. Add sesame seeds, and fry until lightly golden. Stir in honey, cinnamon and vermicelli, and heat through. Serve hot, topped with cream sauce.

## ORANGE ROUND

The oranges give a beautiful color and flavor to this delicate dessert.

Preparation Time: 30 minutes,
Cooking Time: 15 minutes for pastry 20 minutes for filled flan
Oven Temperature: 350°F

### INGREDIENTS

*10oz basic pastry*
*3 oranges, thinly sliced*
*2 eggs, beaten*
*½ cup ground almonds*
*3 tbsps sugar*
*3 tbsps clear honey*

### METHOD

Roll out the pastry and line an 8-inch pie pan. Prick the base of the pie. Cut a piece of wax paper, line the pastry and sprinkle with baking beans (or any dried beans, to bake blind). Bake for 10 minutes at 375°F. While the shell is baking, prepare the orange filling. Put the oranges in a saucepan. Add enough water to cover the oranges and simmer for 20 minutes. Cook until the orange peel is soft and drain the water. Beat the eggs, almonds and sugar until smooth. Spread the mixture in the pie shell. Arrange the poached orange slices on top of the mixture. Spoon the clear honey over all the slices. Cook the pie for 20 minutes.

Above: Taormina in
Sicily.

## SICILIAN CHEESECAKE

Sicily is the home of this irresistible cake, which is
worthy of the grandest table.

Preparation Time: 30 minutes, plus 2½ hours
chilling time
Serves: 6-8

### INGREDIENTS

*1½lbs ricotta cheese, sieved*
*1 cup sugar*
*Triple sec liqueur*
*½ cup bitter chocolate, coarsely grated*
*½ cup chopped candied fruits*
*1 "4 egg" Genoise cake*
*Cognac*

### METHOD

Mix ricotta and sugar until creamy. Remove half a cup and
set aside for top of cake. Add 1 tbsp liqueur to remaining
cheese along with chocolate and candied fruits. Chill
mixture for 30 minutes. Using a serrated knife, cut sponge
cake into ½-inch-thick slices. Take a loaf pan and line with
wax paper. Mix equal parts cognac and liqueur. Dip sponge
cake slices lightly in mixture and line bottom and sides of
loaf pan. (Be careful not to over soak cake otherwise it will
fall apart.) Pour in ricotta mixture, pressing it down and
levelling it with a spatula. On top put a layer of remaining
sponge cake moistened with cognac liqueur mixture. Chill
for a few hours.

When ready to serve, turn out upside down on a platter;
if it doesn't come out easily, immerse pan briefly in boiling
water. Remove wax paper, cover cassata with reserved
ricotta and serve.

## NOUGAT ICE CREAM CAKE

Children and adults alike will love the exotic appearance of this ice cream cake.

Preparation Time: 40 minutes, plus freezing time
Serves: 6-8

### INGREDIENTS

¼ cup ground hazelnuts
16 small wafer crackers
15½oz can pineapple chunks, or
8oz crystallized pineapple
1¾ cups vanilla ice cream
1¾ cups chocolate ice cream
4oz semi-sweet chocolate, finely chopped
4oz nougat
1¾ cups heavy cream, whipped

### METHOD

Grease a 1lb loaf pan and sprinkle the inside with ground hazelnuts. Put 12 of the wafer crackers around the sides and base of the pan. Drain the pineapple chunks (or chop the crystallized pineapple). Soften the ice creams by placing them in the refrigerator. Spoon the vanilla ice cream into the pan and smooth it down. Add the chopped chocolate to the chocolate ice cream, and ¾ of the chopped pineapple. Spoon this mixture on top of the vanilla ice cream. Chop the nougat into small pieces and sprinkle it on top of the chocolate ice cream. Cover the chocolate ice cream with the remaining 4 wafer crackers. Freeze for 3-4 hours, until firm. Spoon or decorate the whipped cream over the unmolded ice cream cake. Decorate with the reserved pineapple. Serve cut into slices.

The port of Marina Grande on the island of Capri.

Facing page: myriad
fountains and waterfalls
greet visitors to the
gardens of the Villa
d'Este in Tivoli.

## MINTED LIME ICE

The perfect ending to a summer meal, when the days are
hot and the sun unrelenting.

Preparation Time: 15 minutes, plus freezing

### INGREDIENTS

*¾ cup sugar*
*1½ cups water*
*Grated rind and juice of 6 limes*
*4 tbsps fresh mint, finely chopped*
*⅔ cup heavy cream*
*3 tbsps light cream*

### METHOD

Place the sugar and water in a saucepan. Stir gently over a
low heat. When the sugar has dissolved, bring the mixture
to the boil. Remove the pan from the heat. Stir in the grated
rind of the limes. Add the juice and stir in the mint. Let the
mixture cool, then pour into ice trays. Freeze the mixture,
covered with foil. When the mixture is frozen, crush it.
Lightly whip the creams together. Stir the lime ice into the
cream and re-freeze. Slightly thaw and spoon into small
glasses to serve.

## FRUIT SALAD WITH RICOTTA CHEESE

In Italy cheese finds its way into all types of recipes. Here
it complements the subtle flavor of the fruit.

Preparation Time: 20 minutes

### INGREDIENTS

*3oz cranberries or cherries*
*3oz raspberries*
*4 tbsps orange juice*
*¼ cup sugar*
*2 tbsps Maraschino cherry*
*3 kiwi fruit*
*2 tbsps powdered sugar*
*3 cups ricotta cheese*

### METHOD

Boil the cranberries or cherries, raspberries and orange
juice with the sugar for 5 minutes. Strain the liquid and
reserve the fruit. Stir in the Maraschino and cool. Peel and
slice the kiwi fruit. Arrange the fruit on individual plates.
Stir the powdered sugar into the ricotta cheese and place a
little on top of each plateful of fruit. Chill. Spoon over the
Maraschino liquid to serve.

The Piazza del Campo, to the right of which stands the Town Hall, in Siena, Tuscany. Overleaf: the steep, terraced slopes of Positano on the Sorrento peninsula.

## CASSATA

No book on Italian cooking would be complete without a recipe for ice cream. This one is especially stylish and perfect for any occasion.

Preparation Time: Several hours for each layer to freeze
Serves: 6-8

### INGREDIENTS

#### ALMOND LAYER

*2 eggs, separated*
*½ cup powdered sugar*
*½ cup heavy cream*
*½ tsp almond extract*

#### CHOCOLATE LAYER

*2 eggs, separated*
*½ cup powdered sugar*
*½ cup heavy cream*
*2oz semi-sweet chocolate*
*2 tbsps cocoa*
*1½ tbsps water*

#### FRUIT LAYER

*1 cup heavy cream*
*2 tbsps maraschino or light rum*
*1 egg white*
*½ cup powdered sugar*

*½ cup candied fruit*
*1oz shelled chopped pistachios*

### METHOD

To prepare the almond layer, beat egg whites until stiff peaks form, gradually beating in the powdered sugar, a spoonful at a time. Lightly beat the egg yolks and fold in the whites. Whip the cream with the almond extract until soft peaks form, and fold into the egg mixture. Lightly oil an 8-inch round cake pan. Pour in the almond layer mixture and smooth over the top. Cover with plastic wrap and freeze until firm. To prepare the chocolate layer, beat the egg whites until stiff but not dry and gradually beat in the powdered sugar. Whip the cream until soft and fold into the egg white mixture. Put the chocolate in the top of a double boiler over simmering water. Remove it from the heat and stir in the egg yolks. Combine cocoa and water and add to the chocolate mixture. Allow to cool and then fold into the egg white mixture. Spoon the chocolate layer over the almond layer and return, covered, to the freezer. To make the rum fruit layer, whip the cream until soft peaks form. Whip the egg white until about the same consistency as cream. Gradually add the powdered sugar, beating well after each addition. Combine the two mixtures, fold in the rum, fruit and nuts. Spread this mixture on top of the chocolate layer, cover and freeze until firm. To serve, loosen the cassata from around the edges of the pan with a small knife. Place a hot cloth around the pan for a few seconds to help loosen. Turn out onto a serving plate and cut into wedges to serve.

The Ponte Vecchio, dating from 1345, is the oldest bridge in Florence.

## BLACK CHERRY RAVIOLI WITH SOURED CREAM SAUCE

*Don't be put off by the use of ravioli in a dessert, it is mouthwatering when combined with fruit, and a cream sauce.*

Preparation Time: 30 minutes
Cooking Time: 15 minutes
Serves: 4

### INGREDIENTS

#### DOUGH

*1¾ cups bread flour*
*1 tbsp sugar*
*3 eggs*

*Large can dark, sweet cherries, pitted*
*¼ cup sugar*
*1 tsp cornstarch*

*½ cup soured cream*
*½ cup heavy cream*

### METHOD

Strain the cherries and reserve the juice. Make dough by sifting flour and sugar in a bowl. Make a well in the center and add lightly beaten eggs. Work flour and eggs together with a spoon, and then by hand, until a smooth dough is formed. Knead gently. Lightly flour a board, and roll dough out thinly into a rectangle. Cut dough in half. Put well-drained cherries about 1½ inches apart on the dough. Place the other half on top, and cut with a small glass or pastry cutter. Seal well around edges with the back of a fork. Boil plenty of water in a large saucepan, and drop in cherry pasta. Cook for about 10 minutes, or until they rise to the surface. Remove with a slotted spoon and keep warm. Keep 2 tablespoons cherry juice aside. Mix 1 tablespoon cherry juice with cornstarch; mix remaining juice with sugar and set over heat. Add cornstarch mixture, and heat until it thickens. Meanwhile, mix soured cream and heavy cream together, and marble 1 tablespoon of cherry juice through it. Pour hot, thickened cherry juice over cherry ravioli. Serve hot with cream sauce.

## MOCHA ICE CREAM

Coffee-flavored ice cream is the perfect way to round off a satisfying meal.

Preparation Time: 25 minutes, plus freezing
Serves: 6

### INGREDIENTS

*2 tbsps instant coffee granules*
*4 tbsps butter*
*½ cup soft brown sugar*
*4 tbsps cocoa*
*5 tbsps water*
*1½ cups canned evaporated milk, chilled*

### METHOD

Put the coffee, butter, sugar, cocoa and water into a saucepan, and heat gently. Stir the mixture until melted, and bring it to the boil. Cool. Beat the chilled evaporated milk in a bowl, until it is thick and frothy. Mix it into the cooled mixture, beating until it is well blended. Pour the mixture into a freezer container and freeze, uncovered, until slushy. Beat the ice cream well and re-freeze until firm.

## STRAWBERRY AND MELON SALAD

This elegant dessert is sure to win approval from children and dinner party guests alike.

Preparation Time: 25 minutes
Serves: 4

### INGREDIENTS

*8oz large strawberries, hulled*
*1 small honeydew melon*
*Juice of 1 orange*
*1 tbsp strega*

TO DECORATE

*Small sprigs fresh mint*

### METHOD

Slice the strawberries quite thinly. Halve and seed the melon and then scoop it into small balls. Arrange the strawberry slices and melon balls on individual glass plates. Mix the orange juice with the strega and drizzle over the fruit. Decorate with mint.

Facing page: blocks of color-washed houses climb the hillside at Positano.

## *AVOCADO CHEESECAKE*

Wonderfully exotic, this cheesecake will delight the most critical gourmet.

Preparation Time: 30 minutes, plus chilling

### INGREDIENTS

#### COOKIE CRUST

*1½ cups chocolate Graham crackers*
*⅓ cup butter, melted*

#### FILLING

*2 ripe avocados*
*1 small package cream cheese*
*⅓ cup sugar*
*Juice of ½ a lemon*
*Grated rind of 1 lemon*
*2 tsps gelatin powder*
*2 egg whites*
*⅔ cup heavy cream, whipped*

#### DECORATION

*⅔ cup heavy cream, whipped*

### METHOD

Crush the crackers into fine crumbs and stir in the melted butter. Use the mixture to line a 7½-inch springform pan. Press it down to line the base and the sides. Chill well.

#### For the Filling

Peel and stone the avocados and save a few slices for decoration. Put the remainder into a bowl and mash well. Mix in the lemon juice and grated rind, cream cheese and sugar. Beat until smooth. Dissolve the gelatin in 2 tbsps of hot water and stir into the mixture. Beat the egg whites in a clean, dry bowl and fold into the mixture with the whipped cream. Pour onto a prepared cracker base and chill thoroughly until set.

#### To Decorate

Carefully remove the cheesecake from the pan. Fill a nylon pastry bag, fitted with a star tube, with the cream reserved for decoration. Decorate a border of cream round the edge of the cake. Decorate with the avocado slices.

Note: sprinkle the avocado with lemon juice to prevent it from discoloring. This is useful when reserving the slices for decoration.

# Desserts

Right: the Palazzo Vecchio, or Town Hall, in the Piazza della Signoría, Florence.

## LIME AND CHOCOLATE GÂTEAU

Italians love chocolate, who doesn't? This glamorous dessert will satisfy the most dedicated sweet tooth.

Preparation Time: 35 minutes
Cooking Time: 20 minutes
Oven Temperature: 375°F

### INGREDIENTS

*½ cup sugar*
*3 eggs*
*¾ cup flour*
*3 tbsps melted butter*
*Grated rind of 1 lime*
*Flesh of 1 lime, seeded*

#### DECORATION

*1 cup heavy cream*
*1 fresh lime*
*Grated chocolate (optional)*

### METHOD

Beat the sugar and eggs together in a basin over a saucepan of hot water, until the mixture is thick. Fold the flour into the beaten mixture. Mix in the lime flesh and grated rind. Grease and flour an 8-inch cake pan and fill with the mixture. Bake in the oven for 20 minutes. Cool on a wire rack.

#### To Decorate

Whip the cream and spread over the gâteau, reserving a little for decoration. Fill a nylon pastry bag with the remaining cream and, using a star tube, shape rosettes to decorate the gâteau. Sprinkle the sides with chocolate, if desired, and decorate with slices of lime.

Facing page: the four-galleried facade of the Romanesque cathedral in Pisa.

## *PROFITEROLES VINE*

This glamorous and artistic dessert looks almost too good to eat, but one taste will soon change your mind!

Preparation Time: 30 minutes, plus cooling
Cooking Time: 40-45 minutes
Oven Temperature: 400°F
Serves: 4-6

### INGREDIENTS

#### PASTRY

*½ cup water*
*¼ cup butter*
*½ cup flour, sieved*
*2 eggs, beaten*

#### FILLING

*1 tbsp cocoa*
*1 tbsp sugar*
*½ cup heavy cream, whipped*
*1½ cups chocolate chips, melted*

#### SAUCE

*3 tbsps strong black coffee*
*1 cup semi-sweet chocolate, chopped or grated*
*½ cup heavy cream*
*⅓ cup apricot jam*

### METHOD

For the pastry: heat the water and butter in a small saucepan until the butter melts. Bring to the boil, remove the pan from the heat and beat in the flour. Beat with a wooden spoon until the mixture leaves the sides of the pan. Cool the mixture slightly and gradually beat in the eggs, beating between each addition (the mixture should be smooth and glossy). Fill a pastry bag fitted with a large plain tube with the pastry. Pipe 20 even-sized balls onto two dampened cookie sheets. Bake in a preheated oven for 20-25 minutes, until well risen. Split each of the balls and let the steam escape; return to the oven for a further two minutes. To make the filling, whip the cream with the sugar. When peaks form, fold in the cocoa. Fill a large pastry bag fitted with a plain tube with the cream, and fill the profiteroles. To decorate and serve: coat a large leaf with melted chocolate; pipe a few curls and a stem onto a sheet of wax paper. Leave them to set; gently peel off the paper and the leaf. Arrange the profiteroles to look like a bunch of grapes on a large serving tray or dish; add the chocolate leaf, stems and curls. To make the sauce: put all the ingredients into a small, heavy-based pan. Stir continuously over a low heat until smooth. Finally, pour the chocolate over the profiteroles.

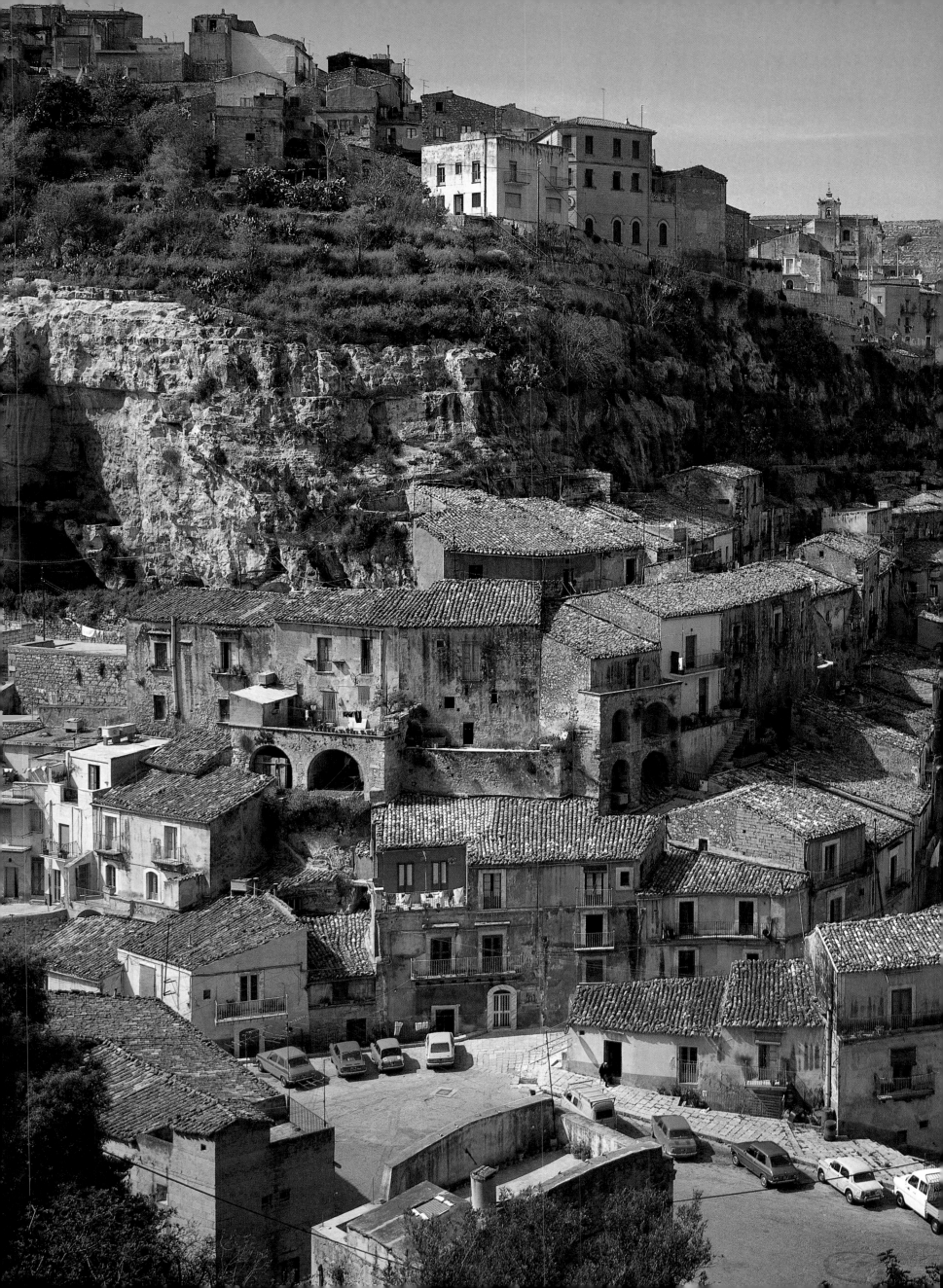

## ZUPPA INGLESE

Fresh strawberries give a delightful freshness to this Italian relative of the English trifle.

Preparation Time: 20 minutes
Cooking Time: 5 minutes
Serves: 6-8

### INGREDIENTS

2 tbsps cornstarch
2 cups milk
2 eggs, lightly beaten
2 tbsps sugar
Grated rind of ½ a lemon
Pinch nutmeg
1lb ripe strawberries
16 ladyfingers
Amaretto
½ cup heavy cream

### METHOD

Mix the cornstarch with some of the milk. Beat the eggs, sugar, lemon rind and nutmeg together and pour in the remaining milk. Mix with the cornstarch mixture in a heavy-based pan and stir over gentle heat until the mixture thickens and comes to the boil. Allow to boil for 1 minute or until the mixture coats the back of a spoon. Place a sheet of wax paper directly on top of the custard and allow it to cool slightly. Save 8 even-sized strawberries for garnish and hull the remaining ones. Place half of the ladyfingers in the bottom of a glass bowl and sprinkle with some of the amaretto. Cut the strawberries in half and place a layer on top of the ladyfingers. Pour a layer of custard on top and repeat with the remaining sliced strawberries and ladyfingers. Top with another layer of custard and allow to cool completely. Whip the cream and spread a thin layer over the top of the set custard. Pipe the remaining cream around the edge of the dish and decorate with the reserved strawberries. Serve chilled.

## CHOCOLATE CREAM HELÈNE

Soup pasta is surprisingly delicious when combined with sugar and cream. The perfect winter dessert.

Preparation Time: 15 minutes
Cooking Time: 10 minutes
Serves: 4

### INGREDIENTS

⅔ cup soup pasta
1½ cups milk
2½ tbsps sugar
½ cup cream, lightly whipped
1 tsp cocoa
1 tbsp hot water
1 large can pear halves

#### GARNISH

Chocolate, grated

### METHOD

Cook pasta in milk and sugar until soft. Stir regularly, being careful not to allow it to boil over. Meanwhile, dissolve cocoa in hot water, and stir into pasta. Pour pasta into a bowl to cool. When cool, fold in lightly-whipped cream. Chill. Serve with pear halves, and a sprinkling of grated chocolate.

Left: the town of Ragusa Ibla is built above a gorge in the River Irminio, Sicily. Overleaf: the Castel Sant'Angelo and (to the left) the Church of St Peter, seen from the banks of the River Tiber in Rome.

Facing page: early morning in St Mark's Square, Venice.

## RICOTTA PANCAKES WITH HONEY AND RAISIN SAUCE

Ricotta is not a strong cheese and is therefore perfect for desserts. If you cannot obtain any, substitute cream cheese mashed with a little cream.

Preparation Time: 10 minutes
Cooking Time: 2-3 minutes
Serves: 4

### INGREDIENTS

#### SAUCE

*4 tbsps clear honey*
*Juice of ½ lemon*
*1 tbsp raisins*
*1 tbsp pine kernels*

#### FILLING

*2 cups ricotta cheese*
*Grated rind of ½ lemon*
*2 tbsps raisins*
*1 tbsp chopped pine kernels*

*8 small, hot pancakes*

#### TO DECORATE

*Twists of lemon*

### METHOD

For the sauce: put all the ingredients into a small pan and warm through gently. For the filling: beat the cheese and the lemon rind until soft; mix in the raisins and pine kernels. Divide the filling among the hot pancakes and either roll them up or fold them into triangles. Arrange the pancakes on warm plates, spoon the sauce over the top and decorate with twists of lemon. Serve immediately.

# FRUIT COUPELLES WITH DRIED FRUIT COMPOTE

Surprise your guests with this deliciously different mixture of dried fruit.

Preparation Time: 20 minutes plus cooling time
Cooking time: 7 minutes
Oven Temperature: 400°F

## INGREDIENTS

¾ cup dried apricots
⅓ cup dried apple
¾ cup prunes
⅓ cup raisins
⅓ cup white raisins
⅓ cup currants
2½ cups strong black coffee

### COUPELLES

2 egg whites
5 tbsps sugar
½ cup flour
¼ cup butter, melted and cooled

## METHOD

Place all the fruit ingredients in a saucepan and cover with the coffee. Boil rapidly then reduce heat to simmer for 3 minutes. Pour into a bowl and leave to cool for at least 10 hours. Beat the egg whites until frothy. Add the sugar slowly. The mixture should be very stiff. Fold in the flour and melted butter. Grease a cookie sheet. Drop the mixture onto the cookie sheet to form 4-inch rounds (the mixture makes 8). Cook in a preheated moderate oven until the edges are golden brown. Remove from the cookie sheet one at a time. Mold over an inverted custard cup to form a cup shape. When set remove from the dish and leave to cool on a wire rack. To serve, fill the coupelles with the fruit compote.

Right: silent cloisters in the monastery of San Domenico in Perugia.

Facing page: the first-century Roman amphitheatre in Verona.

## BAKED STUFFED PEACHES

The contrast of flavors and textures in this dessert make it especially popular with more refined palates.

Preparation Time: 10 minutes
Cooking Time: 25-30 minutes
Oven Temperature: 300°F
Serves: 4

### INGREDIENTS

*4 large firm but ripe peaches*
*½ cup sugar*
*Grated rind of 1 lemon*
*2 tbsps bitter cocoa*
*¼ cup blanched almonds, chopped*
*5 bitter almond macaroons, crumbled*
*1 egg yolk*
*Peach liqueur*
*2 tbsps butter*

### METHOD

Peel peaches, split in half and remove stone. Scoop out some of the peach leaving a shell 1 inch thick. Put pulp in a bowl. Add half the sugar, lemon rind, cocoa, almonds, macaroons and egg yolk. Mix with enough liqueur to form a thick paste. Stuff peach halves with this filling, arrange them in a baking dish, dot with butter, sprinkle with remaining sugar and bake in a preheated oven for 25-30 minutes, or until peaches are tender and still hold their shape.

## APRICOT ICE ROLL

Ice cream is a national institution in Italy, where it finds its way into numerous desserts. Apricots, ice cream and sponge is just one irresistible combination.

Preparation Time: 35 minutes, plus freezing time
Cooking Time: 12 minutes
Oven Temperature: 425°F

### INGREDIENTS

CAKE MIXTURE

*2 eggs*
*¼ cup sugar*
*½ cup flour*

FILLING AND DECORATING

*4 tbsps apricot jam*
*2½ cups soft-scoop ice cream (vanilla)*
*Cream to decorate*
*Apricots, halved*

### METHOD

Beat eggs and sugar until light and fluffy. Carefully fold in flour. Turn into a greased and floured jelly roll pan and bake. Turn out onto a clean cloth and leave to cool. Spread sponge with apricot jam and softened ice cream. Roll up using clean cloth. Place in freezer until ice cream is hardened. Decorate with cream and sliced apricots.

# CHOCOLATE NUT TORTE

Desserts are often reserved for special occasions in Italy, and this delicious torte is certainly worthy of the grandest occasion.

Preparation Time: 30 minutes, plus chilling time
Makes: 1 cake, 7 inches in diameter

## INGREDIENTS

*2 tbsps butter*
*1 tbsp honey*
*1 cup crushed Amaretti cookies*

### FILLING

*3 tbsps cornstarch*
*1 tbsp cocoa*
*1½ cups milk*
*½ cup chocolate flavored yogurt*
*¼ cup hazelnuts, skinned and roughly chopped*

### TOPPING

*½ cup mascarpone cheese*
*¼ cup heavy cream, whipped*

### TO DECORATE

*Grated chocolate*
*8 whole hazelnuts*

## METHOD

Melt the butter and honey in a saucepan. Add the crushed Amaretti cookies and mix well until they are coated with the butter syrup. Press the mixture into the base of a 7-inch fluted flan ring with a removable base. Leave to cool. For the filling, mix the cornstarch and cocoa with a little of the milk. Heat the remaining milk until boiling and pour onto the cornstarch mixture, stirring constantly. Return the mixture to the pan and return to the heat; simmer for a few minutes until thickened. Remove the saucepan from the heat and stir in the chocolate yogurt and chopped hazelnuts. Pour the mixture over the crisp base. For the topping, mix the cheese with the whipped cream and spread it over the chocolate mixture. Put the flan in the refrigerator and chill until set. Carefully remove the flan ring and decorate with grated chocolate and whole hazelnuts. Serve with chocolate sauce if desired.

Facing page: a Venetian gondolier waits for another busy day to begin.

# Index